United Nations Conference on Trade and Development

**PRAEGER SPECIAL STUDIES IN
INTERNATIONAL ECONOMICS AND DEVELOPMENT**

United Nations
Conference
on Trade
and Development

A CASE STUDY IN U. N. DIPLOMACY

KAMAL M. HAGRAS

FREDERICK A. PRAEGER, *Publishers*
New York · Washington · London

The purpose of the Praeger Special Studies is to make specialized research monographs in U.S. and international economics and politics available to the academic, business, and government communities. For further information, write to the Special Projects Division, Frederick A. Praeger, Publishers, 111 Fourth Avenue, New York, N.Y. 10003.

FREDERICK A. PRAEGER, *Publishers*
111 Fourth Avenue, New York, N.Y. 10003, U.S.A.
77-79 Charlotte Street, London W.1, England

Published in the United States of America in 1965
by Frederick A. Praeger, Inc., Publishers

Second printing, 1966

Library of Congress Catalog Card Number: 65-24706

Printed in the United States of America

TO

THOSE WHO ARE WORKING

FOR UNDERSTANDING AMONG NATIONS

ACKNOWLEDGMENTS

I wish to thank Dr. Vera Micheles Dean, Professor for International Development at New York University, for her advice and constructive criticism.

I am also grateful to Dr. Robert W. Crawford of Rockefeller Foundation for the help extended to me.

I appreciate the time and attention which Dr. Abdel Moneim El-Kaissouni, the President of the Conference, and Dr. Raul Prebisch, the Secretary General of the Conference, as well as a number of diplomats, international civil servants and experts devoted to the study of the questionnaire I submitted to them.

I am indebted for the assistance given to me by Mrs. Vivian D. Hewitt, Mrs. Jane Lowenthal and Mrs. Roberta Rothman of the Library of Carnegie Endowment for International Peace.

My gratitude goes to the Ministry of Foreign Affairs of the United Arab Republic for granting me a leave of absence which enabled me to continue my doctoral studies; and to the Rockefeller Foundation for awarding me a Fellowship which made it possible for me to undertake the research for this study.

FOREWORD

The Charter of the United Nations declares that
it is the intention of the world organization "to promote
social progress and better standards of life in larger freedom", and to use for this purpose "international machinery
for the promotion of the economic and social advancement
of all people".

An overwhelming concern with peace and security
has tended to attract more attention to the political activities of the United Nations than to its less glamorous endea-
vors in the economic and social fields. "It is common
experience that political news of any kind is reported fully
by the news media while the most spectacular programs of
economic development and social progress are hardly
mentioned," remarked Secretary General U Thant in an
address in Copenhagen on May 8, 1962. [1] U Thant explained that the 1960's would see a program of coordination in
which the United Nations, the specialized agencies and the
associated organizations would participate. All would mobilize
their past experience and unite their efforts in a sustained
attack upon the ancient enemies of mankind - disease, hunger,
ignorance and poverty - and attempt to lay the foundations in
all developing lands for a more modern and productive
economy.

As a result of measures taken within this framework,
the United Nations Conference on Trade and Development
was called to meet at Geneva in the spring of 1964. A
case study of that Conference is of great interest, since
this was the first time that an international gathering in
which virtually all the nations of the world participated was
held to discuss economic problems. One hundred and nineteen
nations - the rich and the poor, the developed and the developing, those which cooperate in the organs of the U.N. and those
which have remained outside the U.N. - met at Geneva in a
spirit of cooperation, regardless of their divergent political
ideologies, and with the expressed willingness to permit
international interests to prevail over national interests.

This Conference was the most successful step in a
process of development which can be traced back for a
long period of history. The experience of traditional diplomacy in its often changing phases, the experiment of inter-

national organization with its many setbacks and advances had to reach a certain stage where both could combine in United Nations diplomacy.

There are certain elements in the development of both factors - traditional diplomacy and international organization - which facilitated the emergence of the spirit which inspired the Conference and of the international machinery which made it possible. These features - in their ideological and chronological context - will be surveyed here first. It is for this reason that Chapter 1 of this study will analyze briefly the development of diplomacy both before and after World War II; and that Chapter 2 will summarize the role of international organization in world affairs.

To determine the purpose for which the Conference was called, it will then be necessary to examine the needs of the nations in whose behalf it was held. Then, the economic problems of developing countries, and their relationships to the developed countries will be considered.

Finally, against that background, the discussions held at the Conference will be analyzed, and their results will be evaluated.

CONTENTS

Page

ACKNOWLEDGMENTS   vii

FOREWORD   ix

CHAPTER 1   DIPLOMACY

    1. Traditional Diplomacy

       The First Stage   3
       The Emergence of Diplomacy   5
       The Golden Age   8
       Diplomacy in the New World   10
       Transition   14

    2. New Diplomacy   16

CHAPTER 2   INTERNATIONAL ORGANIZATIONS

    1. Before World War II

       The Nineteenth Century   24
       The Concert System   25
       The Hague System   26
       Public International Unions   27
       The Inter-War Period   28

    2. After World War II

       The United Nations
          Organization   33
       Regional Arrangements   40

CHAPTER 3   THE ECONOMIC BACKGROUND

    1. Economic Problems of
       Developing Countries   48

    2. The Developed and the
       Developing Nations   57

CHAPTER 4   INTERNATIONAL MACHINERY
             REGULATING ECONOMIC
             RELATIONS BETWEEN DEVELOPED
             AND DEVELOPING NATIONS

             1. Efforts Prior to the Conference   65

             2. The Preparatory Committee of
                the Conference   77

CHAPTER 5   CONFERENCE PROCEEDINGS

             1. The Plenary Meetings

                The Opening Session   87
                The Debate   89

             2. The Committees at Work

                The First Committee   95
                The Second Committee   98
                The Third Committee   99
                The Fourth Committee   102
                The Fifth Committee   104

             3. The Final Act

                The Document   106
                The Closing of the
                   Conference   109

CHAPTER 6   INSTITUTIONALIZATION OF
             THE CONFERENCE

             1. New Specialized Agency   110

             2. Permanent Body as Organ
                of U. N.   111

                The General Agreement on
                   Tariffs and Trade   113
                The New Institutional
                   Arrangement   115
                Action by the General
                   Assembly   120

3. Conciliation Machinery

      The Recommendation   120
      The Special Committee   122
      The Draft Proposal   123

CHAPTER 7   FINDINGS AND CONCLUSIONS

      Pertinent Questions   125
      The Accomplishment   126
      Permanent Machinery   127
      The Role of International
         Civil Servants   129
      The Role of Experts   131
      The Role of Diplomats   132
      Outlook   135

APPENDIX   137

NOTES   139

BIBLIOGRAPHY   158

INDEX   169

United Nations Conference on Trade and Development

1

1. TRADITIONAL DIPLOMACY

The First Stage

As far back as history can be traced, nations have exchanged ambassadors.[1] Discernible historical beginnings date back to primitive societies where messengers and heralds provided links between clans and tribes. As trade flourished, as boundaries required regulation, as treaties were concluded and notes were dispatched, the need for emissaries to negotiate relations among nations increased. Diplomatic envoys came and went between Egypt and Arabia, Phoenicia and Greece, Babylon, India, China and other parts of the world. These envoys were accredited at foreign courts; and rules were developed which regulated their reception, their treatment and the procedures governing their activities.

To this day, diplomatic customs can in some instances be directly ascribed to such early customs. A lasting contribution to the field of diplomacy by an ancient people was made by the Romans in the area of international law. The organization of archives which permit study and application of precedent and experience and the development of an administrative staff which provides continuity in foreign relations conducted by individual countries and institutions started mainly during the Middle Ages in the Papal and Carolingian Chanceries and at many of the smaller courts of Central Europe.

Historical research has led to the conclusion[2] that the origin of modern diplomacy can be found in the Italian cities of the 15th and 16th centuries, notably in Venice which, in turn, owed much to the Byzantine tradition. Political leaders in the cities which in 1861 united into the state of Italy, attempted to arrange alliances, treaties and other international combinations in order to achieve

a position of power. Since "a certain political system
inevitably reflects itself in a certain type of diplomatic
practice and theory"[3] this purpose determined the type of
diplomacy thus developed. The accomplishments of the
Renaissance produced a diplomatic theory which was efficient by present-day standards, and a practice which
illustrated the defects that to this day must be considered
a liability of the profession. Meticulous record-keeping,
and a system of newsletters which kept ambassadors informed of current events in their home country at a time
when communication facilities were still limited, could
stand comparison with modern methods.

 The inconvenience of constant attendance at the
court at which the minister was accredited, wherever it
happened to be held, in order to watch for occurrences that
might prove significant, was an inevitable burden an ambassador had to assume in order to fulfill the main purpose
of his mission: to provide his government with news. The
difficulties which arose in the discharge of this function
were to some extent responsible for the disfunctions of
diplomacy. Diplomats could not always be very discrimi-
nating in the choice of means they used to obtain information,
a fact which not only made their ethics suspect but - com-
pleting the vicious circle - made their task more difficult
by branding them in public opinion as spies.

 It was during this period of Italian influence on
diplomacy that the ceremonial customs and rules of protocol were most highly developed into a rigid system. Not
only in the Italian cities did ambassadors of the 15th and
16th centuries jealously guard the rank which the position
of their country guaranteed to them. In 1523, the Moscow
ambassador to the Polish court took offence at the preferential treatment of Papal and Hungarian diplomats and
instructions issued by Russia to its ambassadors during
the next two hundred years showed that it had not forgotten
the alleged insult. [4]

 The consideration claimed by diplomats for their
countries at the courts to which they were accredited was
strictly a reflection of the more or less exalted standing
of the sovereign who had sent them and whom they represented. It was completely independent of the social position that the diplomat himself enjoyed personally.   In
this connection it is interesting to note that ambassadors

of that period were rarely of noble origin. They were
usually chosen not for their family background, but rather for their ability to conduct negotiations, their knowledge of languages and of foreign countries, and their skill
in uncovering news. The search for the right man led at
times to the selection of ambassadors who were not even
citizens of the country they represented.

   Although most countries in Europe occasionally
exchanged ambassadors, permanent missions were still
rare. When they existed, they were the result of a new
trend in politics which replaced that created by Italian
influence.

The Emergence of Diplomacy

   Despite the existence of the elements of diplomacy
outlined above, the conduct of foreign relations as a function of government did not become separate and distinct
for some time. It was Henri III of Valois who, in 1589,
recognized the necessity of centralizing foreign affairs by
entrusting diplomatic correspondence to one of his four
secretaries of state.[5] Three decades later, French Cardinal Richelieu, "the King's First Minister", developed very
definite ideas about the conduct of diplomacy. He felt
that foreign relations should not be guided solely by the
demands of the hour. Long-range objectives set, he thought,
should be steadily pursued. Thus, diplomacy would have
to become a continuous process.[6] To achieve that end,
permanent missions were indispensable. But foreign powers
could hardly be expected to trust the diplomacy of France
and to cooperate with that country, unless treaties and other
agreements were strictly observed, and the persons who
carried on the negotiations were fully responsible. This
double requirement called for two prerequisites: the government could not be allowed to refuse ratification of a
treaty negotiated by an ambassador who possessed full
power; and the lines of command in policy decisions had
to be kept clear, in order to give the ambassador as well
as his partners in negotiation the assurance that he could
count on firm backing at home. With this purpose in mind,
Cardinal Richelieu continued the centralization of the conduct of foreign affairs which King Henri III had begun.

But there was still no strict division between foreign
and domestic affairs. The Foreign Secretary was in charge
of some internal matters as well. He did not head the Consular Service, which was attached to the Naval Ministry.
In this respect, the situation in France was similar to that
of England.

In the 13th century, the King of England had one
Secretary, and from the 16th century on two Secretaries of
equal standing. The work of these secretaries was divided
on geographic lines, but not in terms of internal and external matters. They participated in a "Foreign Committee" which advised the King regarding the most serious
affairs of state. In spite of its name, however, this committee prepared for submission to the Privy Council not
only foreign but also certain domestic matters. [7]

In the German states, the foreign service administration developed in a different way. Foreign affairs were
essentially a private concern of the House of Brandenburg,
and subsequently of the Prussian princes. A foreign office was first established in Prussia in 1728 by Frederick
Wilhelm I. [8]

The complete elimination of domestic responsibilities and the fusion of the diplomatic and consular services
was to come in all countries only at a much later date. As
far as the organization of the foreign office was concerned,
however, France was in advance of all other European powers.

France showed an even more impressive lead in the
diplomatic service itself. By the end of the 17th century,
it had established permanent missions in many, and special
missions in virtually all European capitals and other important cities. The centralized structure of that service
was strengthened by the voluminous and detailed instructions
which each ambassador took with him to his post, and
which included the guidelines for his conduct and the policy
he was supposed to pursue. These instructions also acquainted him with conditions in the country to which he was
sent. Central control was maintained by a system of regular communications that kept ambassadors informed about
conditions and public opinion in their home country and
about any change in policy that might concern them. The
lack of a similar system in England during that period -
the early 18th century - was illustrated by the report about
a British minister to Vienna who, at a critical stage of

decision-making, was left without a single word of instruc-
tion for five months, and who complained that no less than
fifty-two successive dispatches he had written remained
unanswered. [9]
    The responsibility of the Secretary for Foreign Af-
fairs in France, as well as in other European countries,
was strictly administrative in character. Matters of foreign
policy were within the sole power of the King. At a time
when a country and its people were considered the property
of the ruler, English, French, Prussian and Russian absolute monarchs could dispose of their territories at will.
Diplomacy concerned itself primarily with dynastic relations and territorial additions of the ruling families. A
network of family relations spanned the European courts
and an early example of personal diplomacy was set by Maxi-
milian of Austria (1493 - 1519) which led to the statement:
"Bella gerant alii, tu, felix Austria, nube."[10] The royal
prerogative to foreign policy was acknowledged even in countries where internal politics were dominated by a group of
aristocratic families, as was the case in the Tsarist Russia of the 16th century. [11]
    Although the diplomacy of absolute monarchs placed
decision-making definitely in the hands of the ruler, and although the personal element was strong, the actual conduct
of foreign relations was entrusted to appointed ministers.
Discussions regarding the desirability of "personal diplomacy" by direct contact between heads of state have been
traced back to the 15th century. Experience with such experiments apparently proved unsatisfactory, and Louis XIV
was known to oppose it. Philippe de Commines, a diplomat
quoted by Nicolson, summed it up as follows: "Two great
princes who wish to establish good relations should never
meet each other face to face, but ought to communicate
through good and wise ambassadors."[12]
    By the end of the 18th century, the development that
led to the establishment of foreign offices and diplomatic
services was virtually completed.
    In France, the law of April 22, 1791, organized the
Foreign Office as one of the six administrative departments
and the decree of February 14, 1793, merged it with the Consular Service.
    In England, the two regional units mentioned above,
were united into the Foreign Department in 1782, and the
first Secretary of Foreign Affairs was appointed to head it.

Governmental administration confined its interest almost exclusively to the ambassadorial level. The staff of foreign missions was selected by the minister or other official who headed them. It usually consisted of members of the family or friends and formed a closely knit unit. First in France, later in Prussia, the conviction began to grow that the amateur quality and the lack of responsibility at the lower levels of diplomacy were not satisfactory. A political academy, established for the training of young diplomats in 1712 in France, was operated for a short period only. [13] A similar "Pepiniére", [14] established in Prussia in the 1730's lasted to the end of the century. [15] The time for the professionalization of diplomacy had not yet come.

The Golden Age

The Congress of Vienna in 1815 brought a new awareness to the European diplomacy.

One of the objectives of that Congress was the establishment of a system of real and permanent balance in Europe. In the early stages of modern history, the European power structure had rested on France and Austria. The major nations had been considered as guardians of the balance of power: their watchful influence was the safeguard for preservation of the weaker nations. But in the 18th century, England, Prussia and Russia became major factors in the European power structure. At the same time, the original concept of the balance of power changed. The powerful countries formed a unit which acted against weaker countries, which often posed a threat to them, and actually took advantage of them. The three partitions of Poland (1772, 1793, and 1795) were a result of that development. To remedy this situation was one of the purposes of the Congress of Vienna.

At that Congress, too, the paraphernalia of diplomatic relations was streamlined and modernized. Questions of protocol, long a matter of heated controversies, were clarified. Harold Nicolson considers the year 1815 the birthdate of a recognized diplomatic service in the European countries. Under the impact of twenty-five years of turmoil and Napoleonic wars, the European countries met around the conference table and this attempt at unity opened new avenues for the conduct of international relations and impressed on the participants the necessity for expansion and adaptation of their own diplomatic machinery.

After a reorganization in 1832 and a consolidation in 1869, the French Foreign Office consisted of three "services" and two "directions". [16] The services were the Minister's Cabinet and Secretariat; the Correspondence Bureau for the receipt and dispatch of letters; and the Protocol Service. The directions were set up for political and commercial affairs and divided into geographical sections. In addition, a division of Archives with a Bureau of Chanceries, and a division of Funds and Accounts were established. This basic structure with the addition of a Translator's Bureau and a Committee of Foreign Services to coordinate the political and commercial divisions remained intact until the late 1880's.

Then, a series of changes was introduced; a Personnel Service and a Legal Bureau were separated from the political and commercial divisions; the division of Archives was merged with the division of Funds and Accounts; a Press Bureau and a Code Service were added. Changes of a temporary nature also occurred. When these modifications proved inadequate, a reorganization was suggested by the Commission of Administrative Reform in 1906 and carried out in 1907. The political and commercial divisions were fused to form a unit with the archives. A new division of technical and administrative offices was added. A Bureau of Communications was created to keep diplomatic missions all over the world informed of current developments; and a Bureau of French Schools and Culture abroad was established.

The staff of these domestic offices of the Ministry of Foreign Affairs was for a long time separate and distinct from the Diplomatic Corps that served abroad. It was only during the last quarter of the 19th century that France, as the first of the great nations, realized the importance of certain changes to maintain close relations between these two groups. The consular service - although less dependent on ceremony and prestige - was not to be kept apart from the diplomatic service; and both - the consular and the diplomatic services - were to form a single unit with the personnel of the foreign office.

Developments in other European countries followed similar lines. The newly organized foreign office departments were almost identical, being determined by identical needs for geographic division, for specialized servi-

ces, for meeting the demands of mass communications.
Differences between the Quai d'Orsay in Paris, Downing
Street in London, and the Wilhelmstrasse in Berlin were
mainly due to the growth of some particular aspect in a
country's international activities. In Germany, as the emphasis at home shifted during the 1870's from agriculture
to heavy industry, those sections of the foreign office in
Berlin which handled foreign trade increased in size and
in importance. States which acquired colonial possessions
opened special units within their foreign offices to adminis-
ter those territories and to deal with their problems. Differences existed also in the selection of foreign office and
diplomatic officials. In Austria, for example, the nobility
of the Holy Roman Empire - aristocrats from Hungary,
from Italy, the Netherlands, Spain - have been entrusted
with ministerial posts. In Prussia, diplomatic service
was not regarded as equal in prestige to the military career, and therefore did not attract young nobles into its
ranks. Only with Chancellor Otto von Bismarck did the
German diplomatic service come of age. [17]

Diplomacy in the New World

        As already pointed out, Europe in the 18th century
was a continent of absolute monarchs. The King's prerogative in the field of foreign relations was based on actual might. However, realpolitik was not the only basis
for the ruler's decision-making power. Foreign relations,
according to the political philosophy of that time, was regarded as an executive function.
        This theory was also recognized by the republican
government which had been established in the United States
on the other side of the Atlantic Ocean. It found expression in the writings of the Founding Fathers and was responsible for the provisions on foreign relations embodied
in the Constitution of 1787. [18]
        In theory, then, the conduct of foreign policy was
a task which the new republic was ready to undertake. The
traditional aspect of diplomacy, however, viewed by the
peoples of Europe and of the colonies, made it suspect to
American citizens. This suspicion influenced the attitude
of the United States in the field of world affairs for a long
period of time.
        If diplomacy was determined by royal family con-

nections, if it was geared to dynastic advantage, then the new republic would have no part of it. If the aim of foreign policy was the adjustment and expansion of borders, if in maintaining the balance of power the weak nations were used as pawns of the major states, the United States did not wish to participate in activities which, it was feared, would draw it into a set of relationships from which it had only recently extricated itself. [19]

John Adams wrote in 1783: "I confess I have sometimes thought that after a few years, it will be the best thing we could do to recall every minister from Europe and send embassies only on special occasions."[20] According to Warren Frederick Ilchman, American leaders were personally inclined to sponsor an adequate diplomatic service, but had to realize that their intention would run contrary to public opinion. [21]

A valid reason which worked against the participation of the United States in European diplomacy was its remoteness from the scene of action. Concern on this point was expressed by John Quincy Adams, "the Department's greatest Secretary", [22] who said: "Ambassadors in Europe can send expresses to their courts and give and receive intelligence in a few days with the utmost certainty. In such cases, there is no room for mistake, misunderstanding or surprise, but in our case, it is very different. Dispatches are liable to foul play and vessels are subject to accidents."[23]

In order to realize how serious a handicap the lack of communications could be, one has only to recall the Battle of New Orleans, fought after the Treaty of Ghent had been signed on December 24, 1814.

But delegates sent to Europe by the United States also faced difficulties of another kind. John Jay's mission to Britain can serve as an example. He was allowed discretionary powers which went beyond the customary limits, since the distance from the home country was duly taken into consideration. Once the treaty which ended the War of Independence was concluded on September 3, 1783, the United States Congress did its utmost to secure execution of the treaty articles; but state legislatures and the courts "openly flouted" certain provisions of the treaty. [24] Such repudiation of an ambassador's acknowledged diplomatic powers necessarily weakened his position at the courts to which he was accredited.

There was also an underlying belief in the United
States that somehow diplomacy was not compatible with
democracy. The history of the Greek city states had taught
that democratic bodies are at a disadvantage in diplomatic
relations with autocratic governments. The failure of
Greek diplomacy has to a certain extent been ascribed to
the fact that ambassadors had to depend on decisions made
by assemblies, while independent rulers, notably the King
of Macedonia, could instantly fit their action to the demands
of the hour. [25]

The staffing of the public service in general did not
receive much attention. Questions of recruitment, selection, training, remuneration and organization were not tak-
en very seriously. For the functioning of a foreign service,
these aspects are of great practical importance. Alexis
de Tocqueville found the civil service in the American democracy lacking in these essentials. [26] To him, democracy
would not be a suitable environment to produce the qualities characteristic for the staff of a foreign office and a
diplomatic corps.

Even more than the public service in general, the
foreign service of the United States had the character of an
amateur rather than professional occupation, and the development which eventually led to the professionalization
of the service was delayed longer in that service than in
other branches of the government. Ambassadors and
chargés d'affaires were typically "politicians in timely
exile, statesmen to be, wealthy campaign contributors,
superannuated generals and journalists", [27] and rarely did
one of them spend more than a few years in the diplomatic
service. However, these remarks concerning the upper
level officials cannot serve as a description of conditions
in general, since even in a professional service such posts
are frequently held by amateurs. It has therefore been
pointed out that the origins of professional diplomacy can
be found only at the secretarial level, for it was from the
secretaries of legations that a career service emerged.

Ilchman's study of secretaries shows that the needs
of diplomacy determined neither the system of appointment nor the standards of qualification. The number of
secretaries usually fell short of the requirements of legations, and ministers had to resort to extraordinary measures. They used their discretion in staffing their missions. The young attachés whom they selected did not re-

ceive any pay from the Treasury, and were not subject
to scrutiny and control by Congress. In this respect, too,
the United States was not unique. Other countries resorted
at the time to the same expedient. But even the secretaries whose appointment was approved by the Senate were
not of the type which would eventually be suited to form
the nucleus of a professional diplomatic corps.

> The few attempts to provide an adequate diplo-
> matic service in the 19th century, particular-
> ly on the secretarial level, failed partly be-
> cause of the prevailing attitude towards rela-
> tions with other nations. Jefferson early dis-
> covered that a popular form of economy was
> slicing the appropriations for the service. If
> minimal relations were standards, issues such
> as personal mobility, the requirement of qual-
> ified secretaries, the recognition of training
> and experience, and freedom of partisan con-
> siderations held no importance. From a per-
> sonnel standpoint, this standard undoubtedly
> dissuaded good men from entering the ser-
> vice. The strength of the British diplomatic
> service of the 19th century stemmed partly
> from the general belief in the importance of
> foreign policy. The American service, save
> for the period 1787 - 1828, was weakened by
> the absence of such unanimity . . .[28]

The philosophy which affected the prevailing attitude was formulated by John Adams who wrote to John Jay
in 1787 that the secretaryship was "one of the few methods
incident to our institutions whereby not only a race of gen-
tlemen, but a class of disinterested, social, artistic and
literary men can be fostered and become intellectual bene-
factors as well as patriotic representatives of our country."[29]

This aristocratic view had been feared by American
public opinion and was in part responsible for the fact that
in the United States the practice of diplomacy proved suspect and was branded as undemocratic.

Only the widespread realization that the United
States could not remain isolated from the rest of the world
but must actively participate in international relations

could overcome the aversion of the American people to
diplomacy. At the same time, a change in the attitude of
public administrators toward personnel principles permitted an evolution of a career service. The above description shows that the development of American diplomatic
service followed its own pattern.

The organization of the Department of State resem-
bled much closer the development of European foreign
offices.

By 1791, the domestic as well as the foreign relations tasks of the Department had been regularized. Thereafter, each decade brought new interests in American foreign policy. Wartime as well as peacetime planning added new areas. As a result, existing sections were expanded. Some were split into various units; new bureaus
and divisions were set up; temporary units were needed
for the solution of specific problems. One of the most
significant innovations - which found its counterpart in
European foreign offices - was the introduction of the
politico-geographical divisions. The increase in the number of these divisions and the subsequent regrouping of
these units reflected the changing balance of power and interests in world affairs.

This process of change, long and painful, led to
the development of the Department of State as an efficient
tool of foreign policy and of the foreign service as a well
trained corps of professionals. Nations which have achieved
independence in recent years, since 1945, went through
similar stages, although their particular colonial experience made the evolution often extremely difficult. [30]

Transition

If it was the Congress of Vienna that consolidated
the traditional diplomacy and made it a viable and respected
instrument for maintaining a balance of power and a measure of world order, it was the Treaty of Versailles which
reflected the traditional diplomacy in its fully developed
stage. As usually happens in such cases, however, the
powerful display of the institution of traditional diplomacy
covered only thinly the development of forces which were
to alter and ultimately to replace it.

The corps of diplomats which in the 19th century
conducted "their business - and Europe's business - a-

greeably and efficiently", "...possessed the temper and
habits of an assured and self confident elite. "[31] Quietly
and discreetly, they acted as chief advisers to the executive of their countries; they represented their governments
abroad; and they furnished the most important source of
international intelligence by reporting back from their foreign posts, using in the national interest whatever "Intelligence, knowledge, discernment, prudence, hospitality,
charm, industry, courage, ... tact" they could muster. [32]
Continued practice and attention to technical details led
to the improvement of these skills.

But the world changed. The time came when the
qualifications of traditional diplomats were no longer ap-
preciated, since they were neither adequate nor sufficient.

Changes had occurred gradually, but the realization of altered circumstances came suddenly. The causes
of World War I and the events which led up to it, considered in retrospect, assumed a sinister meaning. The
postwar attitudes of the vanquished as well as of the victors seemed to condemn the tactics used and the spirit
which had dictated them.

The new influence which during the 19th century
had slowly altered the international atmosphere, and in
the period between World War I and II succeeded in introducing a change in the traditional diplomacy stemmed from
three factors. One of these was democratization in government which made public opinion an important factor in
diplomatic decision-making and militated against "secret
diplomacy". Democratization also called for a change in
personnel practices and a broader base for selection and
recruitment. Another factor was the improvement in communication facilities which brought to every nation a new
awareness of the rest of the world, and deprived the diplomat of his monopoly in supplying reliable information on
the area of his assignment. These two factors fostered
the growth of a third: to see the national interest not in
isolation, but within the context of the interests of the
world community.

These conditions prepared the way for the new diplomacy.

2. NEW DIPLOMACY

Diplomacy has been defined as "the management of international relations by negotiations."[33] This definition gives a clue to the development of the new diplomacy. The technique of management has been modified over the centuries. The concept of international relations has undergone a profound change within the last few decades. The nature of negotiations conducted under these new conditions has also been essentially altered.

The most fundamental change took place in the concept of foreign relations. In the old monarchies, it had been assumed that diplomatic ties and disputes were beyond the concern of the common man. Problems outside his own country did not deserve the interest which internal events demanded. Gradually, as communications improved and foreign trade became more important for every nation, foreign affairs assumed an equal place among government activities. Only recently has come the realization that the conduct of foreign relations is an integral part of a nation's political system, inextricably interwoven with many strands of a nation's life. Matters of internal policy, steps taken on behalf of the national economy, and social development within a country's boundaries may result in attitudes and measures which reach beyond the national scene and deeply influence foreign relations, for good or ill. International developments can, in turn, decisively motivate a country's internal policies. Thus, an evolution of national politics is balanced by a counterpart evolution in international politics. Revolutionary changes in communications and trade are facilitating this interaction, and accelerating the process of change.

Recognition of this close relationship between conditions at home and abroad has inspired reconsideration of how far national interests might be advanced by the improvement of foreign interests. As a result, each nation's well-being and security no longer appeared a self-contained goal, isolated and jealously guarded against interference and competition from abroad. Although international prosperity and the raising of living standards were not immediate aims, national vision became sufficiently enlarged to reduce somewhat the dominance of narrow national self-seeking goals.

Modification in the technique of managing these international relations was both a cause and a result of these changes. The spectacular improvement of communications which started at the turn of the century and continues to this day has been one of the factors which made the change in international relations possible. A broader, and at the same time more intimate knowledge of the entire world became a prerequisite to foreign policy. Once the struggles and the achievements of other peoples enter a nation's living rooms, on radio and television, they no longer seem entirely alien, even though they may be removed thousands of miles in space and a century or more in terms of political, economic and social development. Thus, a common language of human experience is being established. The mass media which permit such direct communication in effect participate in the management of foreign relations. They constitute a force affecting public opinion which no government - whether democratic or authoritarian - can overlook today.

The mass media of communication have been responsible for still another change. Today, the man in the street, who only a few decades ago took hardly any interest in international relations, now considers himself an expert in the field and actually possesses at least some knowledge - if not necessarily judgement - about the conduct of foreign affairs. [34] He is in a position to make practical use of that knowledge by claiming a share in the management of foreign relations through the democratic process of government. Public opinion has developed into a powerful determinant in the management of world affairs. "Open covenants openly arrived at," to use the phrase of President Woodrow Wilson, constitute the instruments which regulate relations between nations, and to an important extent they have replaced the confidential meetings and discussions and the secret understandings which gave traditional diplomacy its restrictive character. Direct access to the sources of international occurrences - eyewitness reports of journalists and travelers, the on-the-scene-cameras of foreign correspondents, televised interviews with foreign statesmen - have deprived the diplomat of his formerly exclusive privilege to provide his government with situation reports. A study of diplomatic practice finds that it used to be extremely difficult for American ambassadors to report and evaluate observations made

abroad since it would have taken exact knowledge of the
State Department's intentions to judge what information
would be considered relevant in terms of policy-making.
The authors of this study blamed this lack of communication for the confusion and paralysis of the Munich period
in 1938-39. [35]

      Communications are thus responsible for a widen-
ing of the circle of participants in the management of foreign relations. A second component that contributed to
this development arose from the fact that a variety of national interests are directly affected by world affairs.
Now that internal politics, currency and finance, commerce
and trade, cultural and scientific advancement are directly or indirectly influenced, and to some extent shaped by
events in other countries, experts in these fields need increasingly to meet and communicate with each other in an
effort to secure for their governments the greatest possible benefits, while at the same time advancing worldwide economic and social development.

      The combination of these various factors has broad-
ened the base for managing international affairs. It has
also altered the nature of international negotiations.
Changed is the spirit in which negotiations are conducted
and changed also are the negotiators. The new element
does not consist merely of the group of specialized experts
which has been added to the group meeting around a conference table. It is true that today educators, chemists,
physicists, public health experts, administrators, military men and a host of other professional and technical
advisers are to a large extent influencing the tone of international negotiations. More important from a diplomatic
point of view, however, are two other changes: one in the
character of the diplomatic corps itself; the other in the use
of what has been called "personal diplomacy".

      The traditional diplomat was essentially an amateur.
This did not necessarily detract from his competence and
fitness for his vocation. "If they /diplomats/ began, as
most of them did, as aristocratic amateurs, the increase
in pressure of business and their own conscientiousness
and assiduity (qualities which they usually had in abun-
dance) made them into grave and responsible professional
servants of their own countries . . ."[36]

      The knowledge of languages had always been an im-
portant prerequisite for diplomatic success. Many of the

other background elements of foreign affairs a traditional
diplomat was able to acquire in the course of his career.
Then, to hold his own in an increasingly complex world,
the diplomat had begun to find it necessary to learn additional skills. The hectic pace of the new era required diplomatic personnel to start each assignment with as much
preparation as possible. The necessity for professional
education and training, and for recruitment and selection
on that basis, had in most countries been recognized for
the domestic civil service during the latter part of the
19th century. The early years of the 20th century brought
the extension of that policy to the foreign service of most
nations and, thus, the basis for a career diplomacy was
strengthened. [37]

The new diplomats must not only be thoroughly
trained in traditional diplomatic skills and encouraged
to cultivate the traditional diplomatic qualities. They are
also trained to acquire at least an understanding of the
special fields which are closely connected with diplomatic
relations in the nuclear age, and in many instances are
given the opportunity to gain expert knowledge in such
fields. Institutions for the education and the training of
diplomats at various levels have been established in many
countries and their curriculum contains such varied disci-
plines as the "delicate dynamics of democratic strategy"
and the nature of foreign labor movements. [38] Similar
schools are being maintained within the framework of international organizations, such as the United Nations International School, and by means of private endowment funds
in the form of fellowships.

The improved preparation of new diplomats for
their sensitive positions had not always led to an improvement of their status and of the share which they had in
shaping their country's diplomatic policies. For example,
the professionalization of the foreign service had ad -
vanced far in Germany before the Nazis took over the government. And yet, there "the Foreign Office, indeed,
was entering in 1933 an era in which its formerly proud
position was to be systematically destroyed, in which its
hitherto uncontested right to advise the government in foreign affairs was to be ignored and its legitimate functions
usurped by other agencies . . ."[39]

In the U. S. S. R., the revolutionary character of
Soviet policies was expressed in foreign missions by the

disregard of professional diplomats, and it took some time
before the international aspects of diplomacy found expression, and the representatives abroad returned to diplomatic patterns. [40]

The lack of attention paid to diplomatic advice and
the lack of respect for diplomatic expertise were not confined to National Socialist and Communist governments.
Craig and Gilbert quote similar examples during the early
decades of this century for France, Britain and the United States. They also refer to the special agents whom
some of the American presidents employed, and to the
packaged groups of experts selected from internal minis-
tries and from private life to represent their countries
at international conferences. These inroads into the diplomatic field by outsiders who usually had less diplomatic
background than the traditional diplomats of the past, may
have been a belated reaction to the inadequacies of traditional diplomacy.

The second new element which entered the diplomatic field and altered its character decisively was the use
of personal diplomacy.

It has previously been mentioned that heads of
states have at times shown an inclination to meet personally, and that, in the past, contemporary observers did not
think well of that practice. In this century, the 1940's
showed a revival of this practice, as summit meetings became highlights of foreign relations. The speed and ease
of modern travel, and the rapid relaying of speeches and
other occurrences at such meetings facilitated negotiations,
and top level discussions have now become an accepted
form of international negotiations. As in previous centuries, dissenting voices can be heard. The misgivings
experienced by proponents of the school of professional
diplomacy were given striking expression in lectures by
Harold Nicolson in 1961. [41] Nicolson pointed out that the
men who today lead delegations to international conferences, being essentially politicians, are as such obliged to
consider the effect of what they may do or say on public
opinion at home, on parliament and on their own parties.
". . . even the most liberal-minded and audacious prime
minister, when he finds himself upon the rostrum, sur-
rounded by microphones, is unable to express all his
thoughts or to indicate how far he is prepared to go in the
way of concessions, or where the frontier of absolute re-

fusal is drawn. It therefore arises that at these modern conferences there is in fact no negotiation at all; even that in the course of their public speeches or responses the responsible heads of delegations and governments may, in their desire to conciliate or affront, commit themselves to promises or invectives from which it is subsequently difficult for them to withdraw."

Nicolson's criticism leads to one of his main objections to top-level discussions: "Diplomacy . . . is not the art of conversation; it is the art of drafting precise instruments in ratifyable form. Good diplomacy is invariably precise; bad diplomacy is invariably vague."[42] Another expert in the field, Lester B. Pearson, as of 1965 Prime Minister of Canada, adds to these objections: "If governments fail to reach agreement through official diplomatic channels, they can go on trying, or, at worst, fail without fury. Political face can be saved by allowing diplomatic heads to fall. But when foreign ministers, or even more, when chiefs of governments meet, with their retinue of press, radio and television companies, with experts, advisers and advisers to advisers, things become more complicated and often more difficult. . ."[43]

But Pearson also recognizes that political diplomacy can be useful, even essential. "It does bring the makers of policy face to face . . . the road to understanding can, at times, be made easier."[44]

The publicity given to summit conferences and top-level negotiations may create the impression that the field of the professional diplomat has considerably narrowed, and that he has been pushed to the sidelines by the politicians. This would be a superficial appraisal of the international situation. Popular imagination is naturally impressed by the spectacle of heads of state assembling to discuss the future of nations; public attention focuses on such occasions.

Yet, these are only few in number, while the work of the professional diplomat creates the background of international relations in its continuity. Since these relations are more complex than ever before, and are spread over virtually all fields of national interest, they demand a well prepared professional staff and very able management. The need for presenting an attractive picture of political, economic and cultural conditions in the ambassador's own country to the public of the nation to which he is accredited

can be crucial. For modern communications expose every
detail of action and criticism expressed in a remote corner
of one country can quickly spread all over the world. Lester Pearson draws attention to the fact that it is this public
relations function which calls for special talents on the part
of the new diplomats: "While the policy makers argue and
orate, the ambassador, sitting alongside or behind his
political chief, may have to keep the press and radio informed of what is going on and insure that the public relations are working smoothly. Then, before the next day's
proceedings, the news dispatches have to be carefully
scanned . . . "[45]

     This observation, although accurate, does not tell
the whole story. The onlooker may see the politician ar-
guing in front, while the ambassador remains in the background. Behind the scenes, the situation is quite different.
It is the experienced diplomat who is familiar with all phases of international affairs which have led to the conference and who is aware of all the details that influence its
progress, its promise of success or failure. It is the experienced diplomat who briefs the politician and who guides
him through the diplomatic labyrinth. The traditional custom of quiet diplomacy serves him well when - content in
his anonymity - he watches the politician from a back seat.

     A discussion of the changes in managing techniques
and in the nature of international relations and negotiations
would be incomplete if it failed to take into account the influence of international organizations. As a result of the
formation and development of the League of Nations, of
the United Nations, of specialized agencies and of regional
organizations, a new diplomacy has been created which
works through international conferences.

     The importance of these conferences and one of the
main benefits derived from them is the combined use of
four elements: the talents and services of professional
diplomats; the interest and occasional participation of national political leaders; the expert knowledge and know-
how of technicians; and the skills of the rapidly developing
international civil service. This civil service has assumed
the responsibility for the routine preparation and the maintenance chores of international machinery and has at times
also taken the initiative in introducing diplomatic action. [46]
It has thus created the framework for the fruitful cooperation of all four groups, permitting a concerted effort in the

interest of international diplomacy.   This development is more fully analyzed in the following chapters.

But first, the operation of international organization must be briefly discussed.

1. BEFORE WORLD WAR II

The Nineteenth Century

Historical surveys of the growth of international organizations customarily begin with a study of Greek or
even pre-Greek federations. Voluntary groupings of urban
communities and amalgamations of city states have been
traced back as far as the third Millenium. But although
some of these ancient associations showed certain charac-
teristics which are considered essential features of modern
international organization, [1] it must be recognized that
there is a basic difference between this past and the present in terms of the underlying concept. The members
of pre-Greek federations were urban communities; in
Greek history, they were city states. Present-day organizations are formed by nations. The concept of the
nation, developed in modern times, determines the character of the modern international organization.

Another aspect which historical studies in this field
often include is the early literature which reflected the
striving for lasting peace and stability among the peoples
of the world. Utopian schemes have had an important place
in the writing of philosophers of many schools. Their in-
ventive imagination was usually spurred by the urgent desire of weaker countries for peace. Such efforts, however,
had little impact on contemporary developments. [2]

International organizations have their roots in the
remote past only in the sense that the beginnings and causes
of every current phenomenon can be traced to some past
development. But the connection of modern international
organization with historic beginning exists in theory only.
To all practical intents and purposes, the forces that produced them began to work only in the 19th century.

Analysis of these forces by various authors has em-

338.91 H123u

c.1

phasized three main lines of development: the Concert system, the Hague system, and the system of Public International Unions.

The Concert System

The Congress of Vienna was not the first conference called to rearrange the map of Europe. The Peace of West-phalia, which in 1648 ended the Thirty Years' War, and the Treaty of Utrecht, which settled the Spanish Succession had required the combined efforts of European statesmen. The number of existing states was then small, and their meetings were intended to take care of certain immediate needs only.

The purpose of the Congress of Vienna (1814 - 1815) was far more ambitious, and it opened new vistas in international relations. The great powers still dominated the scene, but smaller nations were at least admitted to the Congress. And instead of occasional rearrangements of European territories, as in the past, the Conference envisaged a continuous management of Europe. Summing up the change in circumstances, Professor Innis L. Claude, Jr. observes: "Europe was not ready for an institutionalized management, but in practice, the leaders of the major states constituted themselves as a concert of Europe which met sporadically, some thirty times in the course of the century, to deal with pressing political issues . . . diplomacy by conference became an established fact of life in the 19th century."[3]

The topics that were discussed and the areas that were affected by discussion at these conferences spanned a wide range. They were determined partly by the problems and questions which the growth of industry and technology brought to each participating nation, and partly by timeless concern with boundaries and territorial acquisitions, with neutrality and, hopefully, with the maintenance of peace. A certain measure of peace was actually achieved. ". . . we would do well to remember that the 'waltzing Congress of Vienna' of 1815 ushered in a century in which there occurred not a single major international war."[4]

Political alliances were a product of these activities, and on several occasions the participating powers were able to intervene successfully in conflicts that threat-ened peace in Europe.[5]

   Moreover, such important activities as the creation of the Rhine Commission, and the European Danube
Commission, and the attempt to influence European governments in their attitude towards the slave trade in Africa proved to be beginnings of fruitful cooperation in vital
economic and social fields which touched on sensitive problems of sovereignty.

   The Concert system which started with the end of
the Napoleonic wars was brought to an abrupt halt by the
outbreak of World War I. The Congress and Concert era
had proved that cooperation between sovereign states was
possible. It had also demonstrated that such collaboration
does not of itself alter the political climate of a continent;
and that it cannot succeed in raising international standards, or in maintaining a lasting balance of power unless
an agency, to some extent, at least, independent of sovereign states is created.

The Hague System

   A number of conferences held at the Hague sought
to provide such institutional machinery. A legal process
for settling disputes between states by arbitration was the
aim of a Peace Conference held in 1899, and in 1900 the
Permanent Court of Arbitration was established. This
court included in its activities the use of good offices,
mediation and inquiry by governments involved in disputes.

   The second Peace Conference, held at the Hague
in 1907, marched a step beyond the narrow confines of the
European Community. Among the 44 states present were
most of the Latin American republics. At the same time,
the dominant influence of the major powers - always felt
within the Concert system - was overcome by the admission of these weaker republics and other smaller nations.
Professor Claude points out that, "at the Hague /in 1907/
the small states got a strong taste of independence and
equality . . . International organization got its first taste
of the difficulties of solving the conflict between great and
small states as to their relative status and functioning
in the business of managing international affairs."[6]

   The Hague Conferences were not designed to solve
any particular problem that arose among the participants.
Their concern was rather the establishment of principles

and the formulation of procedures that would aid in the
solution of such disputes, and as such contributed notably to modern international organization.

A third Hague Conference was scheduled for 1915
and it was hoped that this gathering would mark the establishment of a regular assembly. However, the outbreak
of World War I in 1914 prevented this meeting.

These two trends of the 19th century - the Concert
and the Hague systems - which later were to prove sources
of international organization - were paralleled by a third
development of a somewhat different nature. The Concert
system and the Hague Conventions dealt with problems
on the governmental level. Although the peoples of the
various nations were deeply affected by the problems involved, they were for the most part unable to influence directly the course of events, and the secrecy which shroud-
ed all discussions of the Congress of Vienna and similar
meetings limited the role of the individual to the submission of petitions. [7]

Public International Unions

But the forces which altered the economic and social life of Europe in the 19th century also had a direct
impact at a lower level, and citizens attempted to deal
with such changed conditions. Organizational efforts to
solve problems created by industrialization and by the
application of science and advanced technology led to the
establishment of public and private agencies. This process was often accomplished by gradual steps. First, the
citizens of one nation faced a new problem by forming a
national organization. If this organization was a private
enterprise, it was later either transformed into an entity
of public law, or was replaced by a governmental organization, pursuing the same aim. At times, both kinds of
organization - public and private - existed side by side for
a certain period until they fused their efforts. This development required no over-all planning or agreement of
intent; it came about without government guidance. Subsequently came the realization that other countries had to
deal with similar conditions, and their cooperation for
specific technical purposes was established across borders. Notable examples of such organizations were the
International Telegraph Union, created in 1865, and the

International Meteorological Organization, established
in 1872.

The international agencies which undertook these
various tasks were profoundly different from the Conferences and Conventions which brought together the representatives of sovereign states. On the one hand, their
sphere of competence was much narrower; on the other
hand, the subject matter they handled was outside the interests and the scope of traditional diplomacy, and often
called for expert knowledge in specialized fields.

The foremost aim of these international organizations was not the administration of their regulatory activities, nor was it the function of arbitration which some
of them undertook. More important was that each of them
acted as a clearing-house for information concerning its
field of interest; that each served as a center of discussion; and that each helped to establish standards and policies in its respective field. It is a measure of their success that some of them survived into the post-World War
II period. The Universal Postal Union, established in
1874, is the oldest specialized international organization
which is still in existence.

Important as these specialized agencies were for
international cooperation in many economic and cultural
fields, the characteristic which made them an essential
factor in the development of international organization was
the permanent machinery which they evolved. For example, the organizational pattern of the International Telegraph Union with a bureau which had an administrative
staff, a council as governing body and a conference of
member states served as a model for international institutions in operation today. The membership lists of international agencies varied. Some countries belonged
to many of them, some only to a very few. There was
also some overlapping in the spheres of their interests.
The 19th century knew of no attempt to coordinate the
work of all functional organizations. The possibility and,
to a certain extent, the problem of coordination and centralization was tackled only with the creation of the League
of Nations in 1919 after World War I.

The Inter-War Period

Article 24 of the League of Nations Covenant pro-

vided in its first section that "there shall be placed under
the direction of the League all international bureaux already
established by general treaties if the parties to such treaties consent. All such international bureaux and commissions for the regulation of matters of international interest
hereafter constituted shall be placed under the direction
of the League."

Here, then, was the over-all organization which was
to coordinate specialized efforts in international affairs.
If the question had simply been one of centralization, Article 24 would have served the purpose of achieving greater
efficiency of operations, reduced cost, and increased ease
in administration, all of which were generally desired.

Political considerations, however, militated against
this approach. Few of the members of the League were
willing to vest in any of the functional agencies the degree
of power which a centralized unit would have to assume.
Many of these agencies accepted operation by majority
decisions, as compared with the unanimity rule which was
a basic requirement for international organizations. Other objections to the coordination of specialized agencies
were either stated or implied. In no case did the membership of an existing organization agree to the coordination
envisaged under the provision of Article 24. Moreover,
a liberal interpretation of the Article itself freed newly
founded functional agencies from the obligation to become
coordinated. [8]

Thus, throughout the existence of the League, each
of the specialized agencies functioned in an independent
fashion and it was only after World War II that a hub for
their activities was created.

The fact that the League did not control the regulation of international interests in all fields did not mean
that the development of the functional agencies was without
influence on the new organization itself. Although their
activities remained isolated, the machinery established
to govern them was adapted by the League of Nations and
developed to the extent that it guaranteed continuity and
permanence of the League's activities.

This development was not clearly foreseen when
the League Covenant was drafted and the League Secretariat was created. At that time, the role of the Secretary General was not defined beyond the fact that he was
to serve as the administrative head of the organization.

His responsibilities and his influence in policy-making
evolved from the international situation, from his personal ability and his attitude, and from the successful combination of these two elements. Neither was it foreseen
by the drafters of the Covenant how important a part the
staff of the Secretariat would play as it developed into a
corps of international civil servants.

The specialized agencies made another important
contribution to the evolution of international organization;
this was the use of experts in specialized fields. The men
and women who participated in the activities of the League
of Nations were therefore recruited from three areas:
from the ranks of traditional diplomacy, as the representatives of the member states; from the international civil
service, notably the staff of the Secretariat; and from experts of many nationalities who contributed their professional and technical skills.

In the League, traditional diplomacy was engaged in
a continuation of those tasks which the Congress of Vienna
had initiated. The outbreak of World War I had shocked
Europe into the realization that the attempts of the Concert system had been inadequate. To the participants of
the 1919 Paris Peace Conference it did not seem that the
underlying philosophy had been wrong but only that the
execution of policies had proved faulty. For this blame
was laid on the lack of communications which had permitted misunderstandings, the secrecy of diplomacy which
had clouded the international atmosphere and the heedless
autocracy of leaders who had failed to consult their citizens. If these were indeed the faults, the necessary re-
medies had to be found.

Diplomacy, good offices, mediation, inquiry, conciliation, arbitration had to be retained as means to set-
tle disputes and avoid future wars. But compulsion was
necessary to use these peaceful means; pressures and
sanctions would have to induce member states to comply
with the obligations they assumed in a world organization,
an adequate institutional framework would have to be established and rules would have to be made to govern a
system of interstate relations. The operation of the system would be guaranteed by the democratic process. The
ideals of democracy, as expressed through self-determination within and among nations, would eliminate the elements of friction which could cause another world confla-

gration.

These ideas shaped the concept of the League Assembly. Each member state, strong or weak, great or small, was entitled to cast one vote, and decisions - except on procedural matters - required unanimous agreement of all the members represented at the assembly meetings.

The broad basis of the Assembly, although it satisfied the striving for equal representation, made it an unwieldy instrument for decision-making, since an analysis of complex situations and an evaluation of countless and delicate details are difficult in a large body. The work of the Assembly was therefore delegated to committees.

However, the Assembly was regarded as a means of introducing a change into diplomatic procedure. The Assembly became a debating body, it functioned as a forum of opinion, enabling statesmen and forcing diplomats to bare in open discussion the points of disagreement. This aspect of the League seemed to promise that never again would secret diplomacy and possible misunderstandings between nations plunge the world into war.[9]

The tradition of the Concert system, with its reliance on the great powers, seemed to be perpetuated in the League Council. Actually, the system established by the Covenant permitted the cooperation of smaller states, even the weakest among them, provided they were involved in a dispute, and thereby emphasized the democratic spirit in the League Council as well. The relatively small membership of the Council, the frequency of its meetings, and the moveability of its seat made it the most effective instrument of the League.

Section one of this chapter surveyed the forces which influenced the field of international relations in the 19th and the first decade of the 20th century. A discussion of developments after World War I has shown that two of these elements - the framework of functional organizations and the concept of the Concert system - influenced the League of Nations. The third element, represented by the Hague system, was also continued in the League. Articles 13 and 14 of the Covenant provided for a Permanent Court of International Justice, "or any tribunal agreed on by the parties to the dispute or stipulated in any convention existing between them." In accordance with these Articles the new Court was established in June, 1922, which, in

the spirit of the Hague Peace Conferences, was called upon
to apply international law in the interest of the peaceful
settlement of disputes.

A new approach to a source of international tension
was made by the Covenant in Article 22. President Wilson's statement that

> Peoples and provinces are not to be bar-
> tered as if they were mere chattels and
> pawns in a game . . . but every terri-
> torial settlement must be made in the in-
> terest and for the benefit of the popula-
> tion concerned, and not as a part of any
> mere adjustment or compromise of claims
> between states, [10]

indicated that ideological considerations determined the
League's preoccupation with the colonies of the defeated
nations. Actually, the matter was much more complex
and involved sensitive questions of politics. Vested rights
had to be respected, the imposition of penalties on the
defeated states had to be taken into account, as well as
public opinion, and the principle of self-determination.
The result was the Mandate System which, all things considered, has been acknowledged as a serviceable road
toward the independence of the colonial people.

The development of international cooperation before
1919 had been interrupted by World War I. The League
of Nations was unable to prevent World War II. The causes of these failures have been the topic of intensive speculation and discussion.

The weaknesses of 19th century movements are easy to ur
derstand. Professor Claude has labelled the 19th century
as the era of "preparation for international organization,"
and its achievements could hardly be expected to have immediate results. Claude calls the ensuing period the era
of "establishment of international organization," and finds
it possible to argue that steps such as the creation of the
League - or for that matter - of the United Nations - are
better adapted to prevent a recently concluded tragedy
than to deal with issues of the future which may produce
new, but conceivably different catastrophes. [11]

The implied criticism of this observation is directed
at a lack of flexibility in the international machinery, at

inability to perceive new dangers and new sources of conflict, caused by preoccupation with past experience rather
than future problems.

Another serious obstacle which frustrated the peace-
machinery efforts of the League, according to some com-
mentators, was that" the inter-war period found 'have' and
'have-not' nations arrayed against each other, mobilizing
total resources to achieve their goals, and exploiting the
limits of self-restraints of a noncoercive international system to seize new territory and power. The fond hope
that an international organization whose substantive actions
required unanimity and whose authority was moral rather
than military could preserve peace and order was shat-
tered."[12]

An important cause for the ineffectiveness of peace-
machinery was also found in the continued adherence of
nations to the multistate system. The concept of supreme
national sovereignty had been retained, and as a result,
attempts to regulate had been confined to inter-state, that
is to international relations.

But the League's inability to prevent World War II
cannot be regarded as the only touchstone of its effectiveness, and its value was not nullified by the outbreak of
hostilities. In retrospect it is clear that the world climate had been altered by some of the League's major accomplishments. Such areas of international relations as
colonialism, arbitration and mediation, concerted efforts
in discussing disputes in an open forum had an incisive
impact on international relations and negotiations which
did not disappear when the League ceased to exist. The
League of Nations was an indispensable step on the long
road to international and supranational organization.

2. AFTER WORLD WAR II

The United Nations Organization

"If we are to build on stronger foundations this time,
what should an international organization have in order to
be effective?"[13] This thought was uppermost in the minds
of statesmen who had participated in previous peace-keep-

ing efforts and who had seen these efforts fail.

The lessons learned from the unsuccessful efforts of the 19th century and from the League's experience were that permanent international machinery and the capacity to enforce the organization's decisions were essential. Previous experience had made it abundantly clear that these were basic requirements for any future international organization. In order to realize these two objectives, however, it was necessary to organize a system that would lend itself to such use. Nations, willing to cooperate in the establishment and maintenance of peaceful world conditions had to devise administrative arrangements which would guarantee a viable international institution, respected enough and strong enough to survive many kinds of crises and to use military power, if necessary, for the protection of the security of nations. Political philosophy, practical and material reasons, national hopes, fears and prejudices - the wide range of considerations which affect decision-making on the international scene - influenced the attitude of governments as to the basis on which the new international institution should be established.

One of the sharpest controversies occurred between the proponents of regional arrangements as against advocates of a universal organization. In Europe, at that time, Britain favored regionalism.[14] But as a result of negotiations in the autumn of 1943, the Moscow Declaration on general security announced the agreement of Britain, the United States, the U.S.S.R. and China to establish a universal international organization. It was the intention of these powers to create a general international organization based on the principle of sovereign equality of all peaceloving states, whose aim would be the maintenance of international peace and security. One of the nations which participated in this project, the U.S.S.R., suggested that the new world organization concentrate only on military security and that economic and social objectives be entrusted to a separate organization.[15] Negotiations at the Dumbarton Oaks Conference ended this disagreement, and the great powers decided on the formation of the Economic and Social Council within the framework of the organization to handle economic, social and other humanitarian problems. At that Conference, the attention of the representatives of the United States, Britain, the U.S.S.R. and China was devoted principally to the problems connect-

ed with the establishment of machinery for world security. On the agenda were such topics as qualification for
membership in the Security Council and in the General
Assembly; the formation of military forces; the transform-
ation of the Mandate System; and the future fate of the World
Court. The proposals accepted at the Dumbarton Oaks Conference constituted the basis for the draft of the United Nations Charter.

    Although the Yalta Conference of February 19, 1945,
is usually included in the steps that led to the establishment of the United Nations Organization, its connection
with that project was only incidental. That meeting of
Churchill, Stalin and Roosevelt was one of a series of conferences which the three statesmen held as partners in
World War II and which served as an occasion to discuss
the strategy and politics of a war which was yet unfinished.
Scholars in the field of international relations have pointed
out that only the swift military development in Europe during the months following the Dumbarton Oaks Conference
made it advisable for the leaders of the great powers to
take up some of the issues which should have come before
an organ of the not yet established United Nations Organization. [16] In any case, however, some decisions were
reached at Yalta which concerned the new organization,
the most important of which was the voting procedure to
be followed in the Security Council. It was also decided
to hold a conference for the establishment of the United
Nations in San Francisco in April of the same year.

    The initial task at San Francisco consisted of a
screening of additional suggestions made to the Dumbarton Oaks proposals for purposes of establishing the United Nations, and was handled by a number of commissions.
The Plenary Session, which retained the exclusive right
of decision, was aided in its task of drafting a Charter by
a Steering Committee, an Executive Committee, a Coordinating Committee, and by a Secretary General who headed a corps of about one thousand staff members. Aside
from the delegates, mostly foreign ministers of the participating nations, these sessions were attended by their
assistants, by diplomats and technical advisers, and by
thousands of representatives of the world's news media.

    After nine weeks of controversies and compromises,
the fifty nations represented at the Conference agreed on
a Charter which was signed on June 16, 1945. This docu-

ment was a modified and expanded version of the Dumbarton
Oaks proposals.

The fundamental merit of the United Nations Charter
is that it meets the requirements which previous disas-
trous experience has shown to be essential. First, it established an organization based on agreement of the major
powers to assume responsibility for world security, with
a Security Council "so organized as to be able to function
continuously" (Article 28). Here, then, was the permanent machinery for peacekeeping which had been achieved
neither by the Concert and the Hague systems, nor by the
League of Nations.

Second, the Charter empowers the Security Council
under certain conditions to "take such action by air, sea
or land forces as may be necessary to maintain and re-
store international peace and security. " (Article 42). This,
as further explained in Articles 43 - 51, was the provision
of sanctions which, for the first time in history, could
hold the promise of becoming a powerful deterrent to aggression.

As a first practical step, the San Francisco Conference established the Preparatory Commission. This
Commission was supposed to use the time needed for ratification of the Charter by drawing up an agenda for the first
meeting of the General Assembly and by working on procedural details. Among the proposals submitted by the
Preparatory Commission was the formal termination of
the League of Nations, which in due time led to the dis-
solution of the League.

In the analysis of the League's accomplishment, the
fact has been noted that the League Assembly functioned
as an open forum for discussion. The General Assembly
of the United Nations followed this example. Since it has
the authority to discuss "any questions or matters within
the scope of the present Charter or relating to the powers
or functions of any organ provided for in the present Charter" (Article 10), specifically "may discuss any question
relating to the maintenance of international peace and security brought before it" (Article 11), and since "the General Assembly shall consist of all the members of the United Nations" (Article 9), the field of political, economic
and social matters that can be brought to the attention of
the world is practically unlimited. That the General Assembly has become the "town meeting of the world", [17]

is its most outstanding feature.

The second organ of the United Nations, the Security Council, has a completely different character. While the General Assembly convenes regularly on an annual basis, and specially at the request of the Security Council or of a majority of members, the Security Council shows a continuity of operation which constitutes such a valuable innovation. The Council not only meets whenever needed, but the interval between meetings is not supposed to exceed fourteen days, in the spirit of the Charter which provides that it shall "function continuously" (Article 28). Under various conditions, the President on his own initiative or upon the request of a member of the Council, of the General Assembly or the Secretary General calls the meetings. In the true tradition of the Concert system, the major powers are permanent members of the Council. But in an effort to expand this traditional great power pattern, six nonpermanent members are elected by the General Assembly for staggered two-year terms. Yet when it comes to voting, the balance of power is weighted heavily in favor of the Big Five, or rather in favor of those five which are supposed to represent the major powers. A majority of seven votes is required for approval of any motion. A negative vote by the United States, Britain, the U.S.S.R., France or China defeats any proposal in substantive matters, and the decision whether a matter is of procedural or substantive nature is again subject to the same kind of vote. [18]

The Security Council bears "primary responsibility for the maintenance of international peace and security" (Article 24), while "the members of the United Nations agree to accept and carry out the decisions of the Security Council in accordance with the present Charter" (Article 25).

Article 26 then proceeds to give the Security Council the authority needed for enforcing its plans: "The Security Council shall be responsible for formulating ... plans to be submitted to the members of the United Nations for the establishment of a system for the regulation of armaments."

A number of committees and commissions aid the Security Council in procedural, in military and special technical matters, in formulating proposals, and in handling situations of particular sensitivity and complexity.

Among the insights gained in the 19th and early 20th centuries was the realization that economic and social differences and difficulties between nations can create friction which is as dangerous to world peace as any territorial dispute. The Economic Council was designed to deal with these aspects of international relations. Article 55 of the Charter enumerates the goals to be achieved in that sphere, and to promote them, Article 56 states that all members "pledge themselves to take joint and separate action in cooperation" with that Economic and Social Council. Various committees and boards were created to carry out the Council's work, and it is the Coordinating Committee which has the task of centralizing the specialized agencies.

The importance of the Economic and Social Council, and the impact of its activities in world relations will be more fully discussed in Chapter 4.

The Trusteeship System which applies to territories held under mandates during the period of the League, to territories which were detached from enemy states as a result of World War II and to territories voluntarily placed under the system by states responsible for their administration was similar to the Mandate system of the League of Nations, particularly in the delegation of routine administrative matters to member governments.

Another area of international regulation which remained basically unchanged was the judicial system. The International Court of Justice continued the tradition of the Permanent Court of International Justice. According to Article 92, "It shall function in accordance with the annexed Statute which is based upon the Statute of the Permanent Court of International Justice and forms an integral part of the Present Charter." That document was the result of the deliberations of a special committee of jurists held in Washington and signed by the member nations in San Francisco at the time of the Conference.

The Court has been involved in four different types of cases: it has dealt with the East-West conflict; the colonial-anticolonial conflict; disputes within the Western hemisphere; interpretations of the legal competence of the United Nations. [19] The selection of the judges is based on the principle of choosing individuals rather than representatives of nations, and this policy has promoted confidence in the impartiality of judgments handed down in controversial issues.

The one element which is the most tangible evidence of the United Nations Organization is the Secretariat. It has been shown in the first section of this chapter that the pattern for the development of an international civil service was taken from the specialized agencies and later adapted by the League of Nations. In the administration of a national institution, such as a ministry, the civil service acts as a continuous link between past and present and future, independent of political changes. Similarly, the international civil service can perform efficiently throughout whatever crises may endanger the effectiveness of the other organs. However, the development of such an international civil service creates its own difficulties. The mere existence of a civil service, recruited from all nations and supposedly assuming international complexion, is problematic. The experience accumulated through the work of the League and the specialized agencies and the constructive efforts made by the United Nations Secretariat have resulted in a "unitary staff, multinational in composition but strictly international in character."[20]

Although there are, in a strict sense, as many international civil services as there are international organizations, it is still possible to speak of one "international civil service" since common standards as well as a common spirit unite the secretariats of most agencies.

In the twenty years which have lapsed since the United Nations Organization was founded, the number of participating countries has more than doubled. Fifty-one nations ratified the Charter originally. Today, one hundred fifteen nations are represented in the General Assembly. Some of these new members were added, as political considerations of the old members favored their admission. But in most instances, membership was acquired upon acquisition of statehood. Participation in the United Nations, equal standing with the other nations of the world confirmed to the newly independent nations that they actually had emerged from colonialism, that they actually were free of outside control, that they were sovereign. The United Nations, based on sovereign equality of its member states, was ideally suited to give substance to the need of the emergent nations for recognition as sovereign states.

The near-universality of the United Nations Organization is a factor which, more than any other, has con-

tributed to its outstanding importance among international
institutions. The United Nations did not replace other organizations among nations, nor did it prevent the formation of new international bodies less general in nature.

The intent of the United Nations Charter was to re-
tain the organizations which had proved useful for international cooperation and to coordinate them wherever possible. According to Article 57, "the various specialized
agencies established by intergovernmental agreement and
giving wide international responsibilities . . . shall be
brought into relationship with the United Nations . . . ."
The Economic and Social Council has negotiated agreements with thirteen such agencies, and this has provided
the basis for their collaboration with the United Nations.

One of these, the Universal Postal Union, dates back
to the 19th century (1874); another, the International Labor Union, came into being when the Treaty of Versailles
was concluded (1919); a third, the Food and Agricultural
Organization, was born in the deliberations that took place
in Hot Springs in 1943, and the decisions to establish an
International Monetary Fund and an International Bank for Reconstruction and Development were made in Bretton Woods
in the same year. [21]

Regional Arrangements

Chapter VIII of the United Nations Charter takes cog-
nizance of regional organizations and states that "nothing
in the present Charter precludes the existence of regional
arrangements or agencies for dealing with such matters
relating to the maintenance of international peace and security as are appropriate for regional action, provided
that such arrangements or agencies or their activities
are consistent with the Purposes and Principles of the
United Nations" (Article 52). Such regional organizations
have never been brought into relationship with the United
Nations, as have been functional specialized agencies, but
the Charter specifically states that regional arrangements
are supposed to be used for the peaceful settlement of local
disputes, and a procedure has been outlined for cooperation with the United Nations organs. (Articles 52 - 54).

The oldest of these regional arrangements was made
between the United States and a number of Latin American republics. In 1899, in Washington, the first in a se-

ries of international conferences of American states was held. The Pan-American Union was founded in 1890 and acted mainly as a permanent secretariat which cleared information, conducted conferences, made recommendations and was instrumental in the negotiation of a large number of inter-American treaties. Nineteen Latin American republics cooperated with the United States in Mexico City early in 1945 in adopting measures which would facilitate coordination with the negotiations in San Francisco in behalf of the proposed planned United Nations Organization.

These were the foundations, leading to the Conference at Rio de Janeiro which concluded the Inter-American Treaty of Reciprocal Assistance in 1947, and ultimately to the formal establishment of the Organization of American States (OAS) in 1948.

What the United Nations Organization intended to accomplish for the world, the Organization of American States intended to accomplish for the American hemisphere. The scope of the organization is limited geographically, but its responsibilities cover the whole field of international relations - not only political but also economic and social conditions. The machinery of OAS was devised accordingly. Supreme policy-making decisions are reserved to the Inter-American Conference in which all member states are represented, with one vote each. The Conference is served by a Meeting of Consultation of Ministers of Foreign Affairs. For special occasions, the Special Conference can be called. The Council of the organization, composed of representatives on the ambassadorial level and at all times available, is the executive organ with broad policy-making powers, prepares the meetings of the Conference and supervises not only the Secretariat, but also three bodies which specialize in the principal fields of interest: the Inter-American Economic and Social Council, the Inter-American Cultural Council, and the Inter-American Council of Jurists. The Secretariat, the central and permanent organ, is the Pan-American Council, headed by the Secretary General. Specialized agencies, serving the interests of the American states, are brought into relationship with the Council, following the pattern adopted in the United Nations.

The formation of regional organizations may be designed to serve various purposes. In the case of the Or-

ganization of American States, the desire to unite the states
of the area was based historically on the policy to exclude
interference by outside nations in matters concerning the
Western Hemisphere, initiated in 1827 by the United States
through the Monroe Doctrine.

Other regional organizations have been prompted
by other needs. For example, cultural homogeneity led
in 1945 to the formation of the Arab League, where the
members have an opportunity to consider the affairs and
interests of the Arab countries.[22] Objectives of the League
were the strengthening of political ties among members,
the resistance to plans for a Jewish state in Palestine, and
the development of closer collaboration among Arab countries in all fields, including economic and social aspects.

Another regional organization was established only
recently to follow a similar purpose - the Organization
for African Unity (OAU), whose aim is to promote the e-
conomic and social objectives of the African nations.

A regional arrangement among Communist countries
was established in 1949. Bulgaria, Czechoslovakia, Roumania, Poland and the U.S.S.R. formed the Council for
Mutual Economic Assistance (COMECON), coordinating
foreign trade and pursuing other economic interests. Albania and East Germany joined subsequently, and a number of other countries participated at times as observers.
COMECON assumed an important role after 1955, when
it was entrusted with the coordination and integration of
national programs of member states.

In some instances, military considerations have been
responsible for regional groupings. The United Nations
system was founded on the belief that it would offer a satisfactory constitutional basis for collective security. The
U.N. Charter has, however, been called an "incomplete
document in the sense that it postpones to the future ...
the agreed allocation by states of military contingents to
function as coercive instruments of the United Nations."[23]
It therefore offers no assurance that basic prerequisites
for collective security will be available. As a result, the
desire arose to achieve collective security through special instruments. With this in mind, the Western powers
created in 1948 the North Atlantic Treaty Organization,[24]
and thereafter a series of other regional arrangements,
based on the same concept. These are the Australian-
New Zealand-United States Treaty Organization of 1954;

the South-East-Asia Treaty Organization of 1954;[25] and
the Central Treaty Organization of 1958.[26]
     The counterpart to these military regional arrange-
ments of the West is the Warsaw Pact of the Communist
countries.[27] It is a multilateral alliance, formed in 1955
by the Soviet Union and seven Eastern-European states,
concluded for mutual defence.
     The rosters of members of various Western region-
al groups indicate that a number of nations belong to more
than one of these regional organizations. However, not
all those nations which advocate regionalism have the same
aims in mind.
     Some observers see regional organizations as a first
stage in the development which will ultimately lead to universal unity. Historic, demographic, politic, economic
and other similarities and common interests of adjacent
areas seem to offer the possibility of establishing an arrangement that could prepare the ground for the kind of
cooperation which is as yet unattainable on a global scale.
The regional organization would thus be merely a building
block in the construction of larger organizations which
would gradually achieve world unity. A second school of
regionalists are content to have regional organizations
ease frictions and tensions among neighboring states and
further their economic and social aims or promote peace
and security. They support regional order as such, and
believe that existing divergencies between sovereign states,
particularly the great powers, will not permit a more universal association in the visible future.
     Spokesmen of both schools recognize that there are
certain problems which do not lend themselves to regional
treatment, since their solution can be meaningful only if
translated into universal terms. This would, for instance,
be true for the problems of disarmament. There are,
however, many areas of activity where regional cooperation can be of great advantage to the participants.
     Some of the most successful regional arrangements
designed to achieve economic objectives have been made
in Europe. A discussion of their organization, following
below, involves another issue which has contributed to
the development of recent international bodies.
     One of the basic principles of the United Nations is
the sovereignty of its member states. It has already been
mentioned that the participation of new developing nations

at the General Assembly has held for them a significance
transcending the importance of membership in an international body, because it confirmed their national sovereignty, and their equal standing in the community of free nations. But this emphasis on the quality of sovereignty is
not generally shared; it is more peculiar to the new nations than to the old established ones. [28] The European
countries have traditionally taken sovereignty for granted, but seem willing now to sacrifice some of its intangi-
ble benefits, provided some more tangible benefits can be
expected in return. This opens the way to the establishment
of supranational organizations, of which some beginnings
can be found in the regional organizations of Western Europe.

These organizations are, in one way or another, designed to deal with economic problems. The most important of these are as follows:

Sixteen, and ultimately nineteen European states
which later were joined by the United States and Canada,
formed the Organization for European Economic Cooperation which functioned from 1948 to 1960. Its primary responsibility was the distribution of United States Aid under
the Marshall Plan. Since the OEEC owed its existence to
measures adopted outside Europe, it was not strictly representative of European regional organization. However,
in the course of its existence, pursuing a policy of trade
liberalization, it fostered inter-European trade, brought
an increase in European production and sponsored the European Payment Union which, in turn, contributed to the
stability of Western Europe.

At an earlier date, a group of European countries
had united in a body which became the nucleus of future
regional development. Belgium, Luxemburg and the Netherlands decided in 1943 to form a custom union, known
as Benelux. This group of "the Three" was later enlarged
into "the Six", when France, Western Germany and Italy
joined the Benelux countries to form the European Coal
and Steel Community. In ideological discussions, the Six
were known to be "Federalists". They favored supranational organizations and were in opposition to the "trans-
nationalists' who, led by Britain, did not intend to trans-
fer any part of their sovereignty to a European Community. [29] Since the French proposal to pool the resources
of the national coal and steel industries was offered in the

context of an organization with a supranational structure,
Britain as well as some other European countries remained
aloof.

The High Authority of the ECSC has actually assumed
some of the powers which traditionally are vested in the
governments of sovereign nations: the right to deal directly with the coal and steel industry of the Community, to
make binding decisions in its area of competence, and to
impose sanctions against violators. The Community's
Court of Justice which is common to all three regional organizations composed by the "Six", watches the constitu-
tionality of the High Authority's decisions. The responsibility for the coordination between the High Authority
and the member governments lies with the Council of Ministers. The European Parliamentary Assembly reviews
annually the actions of the High Authority. This is an effective system of checks and balances which demonstrates
the feasibility of the supranational approach and which encouraged the Six to pool also their atomic resources for
peaceful purposes. Thus, EURATOM was conceived in
1958.

A second result of the successful operation of the
Coal and Steel Community was the creation of the Common Market. While the structure of the European Economic
Community was patterned after the above-mentioned earlier experiments in economic order building, it owed the
scope of its activities to the realization that cooperation
and integration had to be built on a wide basis. Experience with limited schemes had taught that it was insufficient to take into account specific economic and social
problem areas only. It was necessary to achieve a balance of the total economy. ". . . restricted scope, un-
connected with the other parts of the economic and financial system, ruled out any large scale activities and made
it impossible to achieve an overall equilibrium."[30] A
wide scope of cooperation and integration raised other
problems. The economic and financial system of a country is an integral part of its political system; it is indis-
solubly tied to the political philosophy of the party in power. Questions of fiscal policy are key issues in the internal and international policies of each state. Any commitment to a regional organization deeply connected with
these matters will of necessity become a political commitment. And a resulting limitation might easily be in-

terpreted as a limitation of a country's sovereignty. Here, again, was the line which divided the federalists from the strict adherents to national sovereignty.

Since the Six were the power constituting the Common Market, political integration could, to some extent, follow economic integration and certain powers, previously reserved to the national governments, could be handed over to the new organization. It will be noted, however, that the federal character of the Common Market is less pronounced than that of the European Coal and Steel Community.

Those nations which could not accept the idea of supranational organization, led by Britain, are pursuing their economic aims, particularly the gradual abolition of tariffs, in another regional organization, namely the European Free Trade Organization.

The regional arrangements, mentioned above, were made with more or less specific economic aims in mind. But active steps to unite the European countries for more general political reasons date back much further.

When, in 1923, Coudenhove-Callergi organized in Vienna the first Pan-European Congress, the project was considered utopian. The ensuing quarter of a century illustrated the desirability of European unity, while it demonstrated the frustration of any further attempt toward its realization. After twenty-six years, the Council of Europe emerged. Its statute was drafted in 1949 by the foreign ministers of the major European powers for achievement of greater unity between its members, and to safeguard and fulfill the ideas and principles which are their common heritage. The Statute lists among the Council's aims human rights and unity in legal, economic and social matters. There were ten original members, [31] but the open-ended membership policy resulted in the admission of many additional participants. It has been considered the great merit of the Council that it offered the opportunity of creating and formulating a "European Opinion" that could guide the policies of national governments. The powers of discussion and recommendation given the "Consultative Assembly" are limited only to the extent that the subject considered must be approved by the member governments through the Committee of Ministers. The latter consists of the ministers of foreign affairs of the member countries.

An economic integration program, in some respects similar to the European Economic Community, has been undertaken by developing states in South America. The Latin American Free Trade Association (LAFTA) was established in 1960 by the Montevideo Treaty, and as of the beginning of 1965, it included Argentina, Brazil, Chile, Colombia, Ecuador, Mexico, Paraguay, Peru and Uruguay. The principal aims of LAFTA are stated in Articles 3 and 14 of the Treaty Establishing a Free Trade Area and Instituting the Latin American Free Trade Association: to "gradually eliminate, in respect to substantially all their reciprocal trade, such duties, charges and restrictions as may be applied to imports of goods originating in the territory of any Contracting Party," and to "insure the continued expansion and diversification of reciprocal trade."

A study of regional organizations reveals that economic blocs have been forming in different areas of the world. Each bloc is a self-contained unit, seeking to promote the interests of its member states by coordinating their political, economic, social and other activities. These aims are often pursued without consideration to the interests of similar blocs, established by other countries. It may well be that regionalism will ultimately prepare the road to globalism. What regional arrangements with economic aims have accomplished so far, however, is merely to substitute blocs of countries for individual nations in the competitive struggle for economic advantages in the world market.

A more universal approach to the solution of economic problems has been attempted by other international and specialized organizations which handled particular phases of the economic and social life of member countries.

In order to evaluate the work done by international agencies in the economic field, the special economic problems which threaten world-wide cooperation must be understood. They will be briefly surveyed in the next chapter.

CHAPTER **3** THE ECONOMIC
          BACKGROUND

1. ECONOMIC PROBLEMS
OF DEVELOPING COUNTRIES

The majority of the nations occupying the greater
part of the world belong to a group which, until 1961, was
called "underdeveloped", but which is now hopefully being referred to as "developing" countries. [1]
The term itself implies a frame of reference. To
be "underdeveloped", these countries must be compared
with something more developed; to be "developing", they
must be on their way to a more desirable stage of perfec-
tion. It is assumed, then, that there is a basic pattern
which provides a yardstick for the degree of advance toward
a goal. The aim of the developing nations is to achieve
the stage of development which exists in the developed
countries. The yardstick by which they measure their
achievement or lack of achievement is usually that of annual national income.
This selection of the per capita amount of national
income which a country can produce may imply a rather
materialistic approach. It seems to equate economic development with total development and to disregard spiritual achievement and culture. Nevertheless, when the practical problems of developing countries are discussed on a
worldwide scale, spiritual values cannot be compared or
considered except where they have a bearing on the advancement or the retardation of political, social, cultural
or other values.
Yet, the mathematics of the income comparison are
also debatable. It has been pointed out that the national
currency of the various countries whose income is compared, is converted into dollars, but that this is done at
rates which often fail to reflect the real cost of goods.
On that basis, it has been suggested that what should be
compared is not money, but the amount of work required
to purchase certain types of goods. [2]
Such more or less accurate ways of comparison may

result in different methods of grading among developing
countries. Yet, whatever method is used, all of them reveal the dividing line between the two sections of the world -
the countries which have been enjoying sovereignty for
a long period of time, have gone through the industrial revolution, and are now called the "rich"; and the others,
the "poor", many of which have only recently emerged
from colonial domination by Western nations.

It is a truism that the economy of a country influ-
ences and at the same time is influenced by every other
aspect of a nation's life. In the developing countries this
influence is greatly expanded. If an effort is made to remedy the situation which exists in the economic field, it
will be found that no real advance can be made unless some
cultural or social conditions have been altered as well;
but such changes may be quite out of reach for the nation
whose economy cannot provide the means to undertake
them. One example is the need for qualified labor to increase production; a certain minimum of schooling to a-
chieve the ability to read and follow instructions can not
be acquired if the country is too poor to provide education; yet there will be no funds to raise the level of education unless labor is made more productive. Comparable
relations of interdependence, resulting in similar vicious
circles, exist between economic, social and political fields.
For example, the overpopulation of some countries which
poses almost insurmountable economic obstacles to development has been created by advances in the field of
public health. Thus, paradoxical as it may seem, progress
in one respect, far from yielding an over-all benefit, may
create unforeseen new hardships.

Barbara Ward approaches these difficulties[3] by analyzing the impact of the developed world on the underdeveloped areas. She speaks of three Western revolutions
affecting the economy for which the emergent nations were
not sufficiently prepared: the materialistic revolution - the
drive toward material advance and change which met with
reluctant response only; the biological revolution - the
population explosion - which reduced the possibilities of
savings and capital accumulation; these, in turn, are essential for the third revolution - the application of capital and science to all processes of production. Since any
increase in the national income requires a threefold investment in production tools, equipment and so on, [4] the

consequences of the biological revolution endanger the chances for economic growth which the development of savings, science and technology may bring about and which ordinarily would be stimulated by the mutual cumulative propagation of science and industry.[5] Because of this interaction, a total approach to the development problems of a nation is necessary.

It is now accepted that no country can exist in isolation, that in one world every nation is an integral part. Yet, the problems of developing countries are often still treated as if they had no connection with the world of the rich.

The developed countries are aware of the fact that "most of the dilemmas of the underdeveloped areas have been stirred up by Western impact."[6] This statement contains nothing more than the expression of a causal connection. The contact of underdeveloped nations with developed nations has made an impression on the former, and it started a process of changes which, at least for the underdeveloped nations, brought difficult problems. The statement does not touch on the question why the poor nations were poor before colonialization or are poor today, why they have remained at a certain stage of development while another part of the world - a very small part - has progressed much further. It is doubtful that the entire blame for their poverty can be fixed on the affluent nations or even on those powers which had colonies since among the underdeveloped nations are some which were never even subjected to colonial rule.[7]

Whatever the reasons for the difference in economics, there came gradually the realization that inequality of opportunity could no longer be tolerated by the rich or by the poor nations.

A report by a group of experts, appointed by the Secretary General of the United Nations, indicated as early as 1951[8] that it would require the cooperation of the developing countries themselves as well as of the developed countries, and also of the international organizations if the problem of equal economic opportunity was to be successfully attacked.

The recommendations which international experts worked out were directed, in the first instance, to the governments of the underdeveloped countries, with the suggestion that they study preconditions and the institutional framework required for economic development and promote more complete and more efficient utilization of their own economic resources. Another set of recommendations was addressed to the developed nations. These called for the adoption of certain economic policies that would benefit the developing countries. A third set of recommendations went to the United Nations and the specialized agencies for assistance on both levels, especially on the field of finance. The work done by the International Organizations will be discussed in Chapter 4.

The steps taken by the governments of the rich and of the poor nations were closely connected and in most areas interdependent. The developed nations expressed a great willingness to extend assistance. Whether such benefits were extended in the form of aid or of trade, they were based on certain plans which the developed countries deemed the advisable course of action for the new nations. Some of these plans were workable at the particular stage of development at which they were introduced; others, often conceived in the image of the established economy of the industrialized nation, failed. "There is a tendency among some engineers to believe that the 'best practice' in the United Kingdom, Switzerland or the United States is the best practice everywhere," wrote Professor Eckaus. ". . . there are tendencies also in business organizations which would lead to the implementation of inappropriate technologies in the less developed areas."[9]

In any case, once these assistance plans were put into action, the developing nations were assumed to be equipped for participation in the world market. Not much further effort was made to consider their needs and special weaknesses. The developed countries set their own economic aims and executed their own economic policies regardless of the impact on the developing economies. This procedure at times not only deprived the poor nations of the benefits derived from assistance, but also jeopardized some of their indigenous efforts. For example, the technical aid extended to some developing countries to improve their rubber production has sometimes been offset by the fact that industrialized nations substituted synthetics for rubber in their own economy.[10] Protection accorded to some foodstuff commodities, such as sugarbeets or meat, within the economy of a number of developed countries virtually closed the world market to developing nations which produced the same items at a lower cost.

This failure to integrate the economies of the underdeveloped countries into the world economy, and disregard of their trade needs once a certain measure of aid
has been extended to them, was underlined by the fact that
an exception was made to the rule. Developed countries
have shown a tendency to unite for various aims. Among
the regional arrangements, the European Economic Community represents a promising effort toward integration
and synchronization of economic policies and resources.
Although EEC was conceived as an arrangement among
neighboring countries, the Six showed willingness to admit
to their Common Market some countries outside the Western European region as "associated states", provided such
territories were or had at one time been dependents of a
member country. This made a special form of association possible between Western Europe and a number of
African nations.

Here was an opportunity for developing countries to
participate in a cooperative scheme with developed countries. This was the first step toward real integration, on
a level with the established nations. Since such integration between Europe and Africa was reserved for a small
group of developing nations who thus had the privilege of
access to European markets, this served to reveal the lack
of opportunity for the rest of the poor world, and even
weakened the position of other developing countries. The
logical result was the attempt of some developing nations
to form regional arrangements of their own.

Sidney Dell, an English economist, described an early common market experiment in East Africa, and he came
to the conclusion that the benefit derived was very uneven
and varied considerably in its value for the participants. [11]
The advantages which can be expected from such schemes
for the underdeveloped countries are generally very limited, since certain basic similarities in their economic problems do not lend themselves to the establishment of an over-
all balance of combined economies. A survey of economic problems, peculiar to developing nations, will explain this difficulty.

It has been mentioned previously that the expectation
of economic development arises as a result of comparison
between conditions in the developed and the underdeveloped
countries. This comparison means that standards are be-

ing introduced which are new to the developing economy.
The old standards were part of the old economic and social order, and any sudden change finds the population
unprepared, and possibly unwilling to conform to such
change. Yet, adaptation is necessary not only as a technical aspect of change but as a psychological prerequisite
to create the atmosphere in which economic changes can
be made. [12] Psychological problems have been serious
and long lasting.

There is, to begin with, the basic difficulty of con-
ceiving the possibility of progress as such and, resulting
from it, the inability to see its merit. Where spiritual
values are more desirable than worldly possessions and
where prestige is independent of material wealth, it seems
hardly worthwhile to expand efforts to achieve the kind of
progress which appears to be the attainment of an alien
Western people. But even if the fruits of an effort toward
industrial progress seem attractive, a history of oppres-
sion whether under colonial or indigenous rule, conditioned
many of the underdeveloped people to doubt that they themselves would benefit by the change. And experience gained
under a legal order that safeguarded the rights of landown-
ers without protecting those of the tenants and laborers
has the same effect. This is one of the instances, where the
connection between political and social conditions on the
one hand, and economic problems on the other hand, becomes very clear. Another problem is the caste system
that prevented cooperation of the entire developing population toward economic goals, depriving large groups of participation in any economic improvement and depriving the
economy of the benefits it could derive from these groups.

Attempts to overcome these difficulties of the developing nations by themselves are slow, with many relapses,
and may set one part of the population against the other.
The one factor which can ease the painful process of adjustment is leadership. Leaders who have the confidence
of their people and the vision and imagination to know the
goals which must be sought can unite their people and con-
vince them that economic development is desirable and
that work to achieve it is worthwhile.

The next step is planning. Even if it is not possible
to determine at the earliest stage what the complete plan
of development will call for, [13] the government of the developing nation must have a clear conception of its imme-

diate aim and of the resources that are at its disposal for
pursuing them. Here arises the second initial problem. In
order to plan the best use of existing resources, there
must be knowledge what these resources are. This knowledge is for the most part lacking in the developing countries. There are, as a rule, no reliable statistics to determine the basic facts of both human and material resources. Also lacking are surveys which could provide a picture of existing laws and customs that influence saving and
investment habits, economic relationships between the private and the public sector of the various branches of the
economy, and data which reveal the current use of resources. Gradually, the underdeveloped nations, utilizing the
experience gained by the developed nations and imparted
to them, undertake these surveys and prepare statistics.
They are then ready to tackle the main problem: to devise
a plan for reducing poverty.

A study conducted in this area of research has suggested that the low level production is directly responsible for poverty in underdeveloped countries; that it derives
from a low level of technical and organization skill residing
in the human factor of production and from a small quantity of the complementary factors of production, i. e., the
total of land and capital; and that this insufficiency in human
and material resources is, in turn, caused by geographical, political and social facts. Since the geographical, political and social facts vary, the specific problems of each
country also vary; but the basic description fits fairly all
developing countries. [14]

The human factor, once the precondition of psychological adjustment is under way, can be expected to improve as a result of higher standards of living and of public health, and of increased educational opportunities.
Since these developments are financially dependent on the
success of national production, improvement of the material factors is of primary importance.

Although agriculture has in the past been the most
widespread occupation in practically all underdeveloped
countries, land as a resource has been scarce. The feud-
al or quasi-feudal pattern which existed in many parts of
the world has brought benefits to a relatively small group,
and has set production goals in the interest of the landown-
ers. Land reforms and land settlement projects have been
designed to deal with this problem, to bring valuable land

resources into more productive use. To increase production decisively, however, a change in the traditional system of agriculture has been necessary through the use of
modern tools and machinery, by the scientific application
of agricultural research, and an appropriate change in
crops, as well as the introduction of up-to-date market-
ing and financing facilities. [15]

To make such changes, other sectors of the economy
have to contribute their share. Lack of capital usually causes a serious problem which blocks development.

It is not only poverty that jeopardizes attempts to
stimulate investment. [16] Wealth which exists in underdeveloped countries often takes the form of hoards of gold,
of buried treasures and occasionally of foreign currency,
considered more reliable than the country's own money.
This distrust in the native economy is also expressed by
the tendency of wealthy persons in some underdeveloped
countries to keep funds on deposit with Swiss and other foreign banks. Here again one sees the close tie between economic and political problems. Distrust of the political
system, however, is not the only cause which deprives the
economy of resources. Savings in banks and other institutions, and investment in enterprises do not belong to the
traditional pattern of underdeveloped nations, mainly because the opportunity was not offered by the traditional
society, and it takes more than the promise of high return
on capital to alter these habits. Government action on the
part of the developing country is required to stimulate private investment and to introduce public investment. [17] Fiscal policy must take into account the fact that savings are
the main source of domestic capital formation, and that
the rate of savings tends to rise with increased per capita
income. A group of experts, appointed by the Secretary
General of the United Nations in 1951, investigated measures which may act as incentives to private investment in
developing countries. [18]

Even if some new nations are able to conquer their
dislike of outside participation in their economies and to
admit foreign capital, political and economic conditions
have to be sufficiently attractive and confidence-inspir-
ing, and guarantees have to be offered to encourage foreign investment.

With a low level of skill and practically no capital
ready to invest, the population of an underdeveloped coun-

try is mainly dependent on its natural resources. The out-
put of agriculture and of mining, produced in the traditional
manner, is generally used for internal consumption. Any
demand for foreign goods can be satisfied only through the
exports of these primary commodities, which can bring
foreign currency. This is true not only of consumer goods
which, in the first stages, are of minor importance, but
also of the tools of industrialization and more efficient production. The development of the economy is therefore dependent on the results of foreign trade.

At a later stage in development, when the population
has had the opportunity to acquire education, skills and
technics, when local private and public investment have
been stimulated and foreign investment has been attracted,
foreign trade may become only one of the factors - not
the principal one, as is often the case today - which determine the rate of growth.

At that later stage, diversification of the economy
may have advanced far enough to permit the establishment
of a gainful exchange of goods with other developing countries, and regional arrangements may bring advantages.
During the first crucial years and decades, however, when
every forward step is painfully slow, since not only material resources are scarce, but the political atmosphere
has not yet become favorable to change, the main emphasis is on trade with the developed countries.

The group of experts who, in 1951, studied measures
needed for the development of underdeveloped countries, [19]
found that the ratio of exports to the national income of underdeveloped countries as a whole appeared to be about 20
per cent. They concluded that favorable and stable terms
of trade are therefore a matter of utmost importance to
developing countries. And they found that, "the position
of underdeveloped countries in respect to their export proceeds and terms of trade is traditionally precarious and
vulnerable." Among the causes of this situation are the
facts that exports consist mainly of primary commodities,
that these commodities are subject to violent swings in
prices, and that the decrease in unit price can, as a rule,
not be compensated by increased export. To keep the economy going at a steady rate and to maintain the desired level of imports, loans have to be contracted. Increasing indebtedness, caused by market fluctuations, will then develop into yet another problem for the developing nations.

A variety of counter-measures is available to the developing nations to overcome the ill effects of fluctuating world markets. [20] Their effectiveness is problematic, and even more so is, however, the ability of the government to implement such legislation. This is one of the areas of development where the developing countries must rely heavily on the cooperation of the developed nations and where aid proves of merely temporary help. Cooperation among developing nations will rarely bring relief, since imports and exports are not likely to complement each other. It is chiefly the trade policy of the developed countries which can enable the developing nations to maintain their import capacity without increasing their indebtedness. "Trade policy is among the important instruments of economic control, and what form it takes is of significance to today's underdeveloped countries. "[21]

A number of the problems mentioned in this chapter can be approached successfully through technical assistance. This is true, for instance, of the training of technicians, and the application of scientific methods to agriculture. In some instances, only foreign aid can bring prompt relief which permits the underdeveloped country to concentrate on future rather than immediate needs. For long-term economic development, however, the participation of a developing country in international trade is indispensable. The chances of developing countries to play an integrated role in the world market are slim, unless the developed nations cooperate by considering not only their own interests, but also those of their less affluent partners.

2. THE DEVELOPED AND THE DEVELOPING NATIONS

The concept of economic aid among nations is of recent origin. It owes its existence to the emergency situation which was the result of World War II, and such aid was conceived as an emergency measure. Economic strength and financial independence were restored to the war-damaged European nations and once these objectives were achieved, the Marshall Plan had served its purpose; aid ceased and the beneficiaries continued their previous economic development which political turmoil, war and the aftermath of war had interrupted.

The background of the Marshall Plan program was composed of various elements. There were the fundamental humanitarian considerations, the compassion of Americans who, upon the liberation of European countries from Nazi rule, had found unspeakable suffering and felt morally obliged to relieve it. [22] There was also the desire to demonstrate to the conquered nations that the victors did not blame the people but the leaders, that they had not meant to wage war against the people and that there was no thought of revenge. It was essential to create an atmosphere that would promote international cooperation rather than breed plans for future wars. There was still a third consideration, more specific and political in its nature: only two powerful nations had emerged from World War II - the United States and the U.S.S.R. The two vied with each other to develop the largest possible sphere of influence within the European continent. To the United States, aid seemed a certain way of making friends and, as Eugene R. Black observed in 1960, "economic aid, particularly in the United States, is still talked of primarily as a tactical weapon in the cold war."[23]

The competition between the two powers was not confined to the European countries. During the subsequent twenty years, as new nations emerged in Africa and in Asia, the world watched how these uncommitted governments were faced with a choice: to make an attempt at remaining uncommitted, to join the Soviet bloc, or to adopt the ways of Western democracy. It was a serious dilemma for each one of these new nations, since they had hardly had the opportunity to make a judgement for themselves. Wrestling with fundamental difficulties of economic, social and political nature, they had not had an opportunity to know their own aims. It was not fair to expect their leaders to make instantaneous decisions. The most diplomatic way was to postpone the choice and, if this failed, to choose the most expedient way which promised to bring favorable results quickly.

This situation gave rise to an unprecedented increase in economic aid in a competitive spirit.

Regardless of the politics involved, there are inherent difficulties in any program of foreign economic aid.

The experience acquired by the United States during the administration of the Organization for European Eco-

nomic Cooperation could be of little help in programs for
developing countries.   Eugene R. Black has pointed out
that

> The governments participating in the Marshall
> Plan shared a common heritage and a common
> clearly defined predicament.   The economic and
> political aims of one nation found, if not a ready
> response, at least a sympathetic hearing in the
> others.   A clear, limited and complete objective
> presented itself . . . It was possible to measure
> usefully, if not entirely precisely, the economic
> resources needed to achieve that objective . . .[24]

In the underdeveloped countries, the United States
dealt with unknown quantities.   Before a plan could even
be conceived to determine needs and priorities, the existing situation had to be explored and evaluated.   Literature
on the initial phase of American foreign aid describes some
of the basic shortcomings: that the first distributors of
economic and technical assistance created the type of the
"ugly American" by their sense of superiority, their limited understanding of native psychology and indigenous society, their lack of adaptability and, at best, their attitude
of condescension.   As often happens, this initial impression outlasted in the memory of some developing countries
the vastly improved performance of later arrivals.
American economic experts extending aid had to learn
their lessons in other respects as well.   Once they had surveyed the situation and discovered the needs, projects were
planned and executed.   It then happened that such projects
did not always fit into the economy, that their integration
created friction.   National pride, a sense of competition
with other developing nations, a variety of sentiments and
social considerations may prompt a new nation to seek the
fulfillment of an ambitious dream for which the necessary
background or even the urgent need does not exist.   If the
country which possesses the power to extend aid lends its
assistance uncritically, without a sense of responsibility
to see that scarce resources are used economically and
in the interest of long-range development, these efforts are
not only wasted but may jeopardize later urgent improvements.   It is the valuable contribution of the foreign economist and administrator of aid to "illuminate the choi-

ces"[25] - the proper choices - that will maximize the available economic benefits, although the highly charged political atmosphere will limit the administrator's possibilities.

Wrong moves in this direction led to the realization that nation-wide economic planning is the first logical step; that such a development plan creates the framework for programs and projects; and that, as a third step, the investments have to be chosen which will permit effective implementation.[26]

Both the public and the private sector of the American economy participate in this program. Government aid is extended through bilateral agreements in the form of grants and loans, and through technical assistance and private aid through foreign investment. Foreign assistance under governmental economic assistance programs by grants and loans for the years 1948 through 1962 amounted to 33,571 million dollars.[27] For the years 1954 through 1959, the total amount which the United States government has given to developing countries was close to 6,000 million dollars in grants and 1,500 million dollars in loans; American private capital that went to developing countries during the period 1956 through 1959 amounted to more than 4,600 million dollars.[28]

This substantial investment in a policy of good will, designed to encourage the belief in the democratic way of life and its economy, has had mixed results. "The values of freedom and democracy cannot be sold like soap; nor are they the necessary result of economic development. People in the West came to respect these values only gradually over many years. If respect for them is to spread among the people of the underdeveloped world, the West must be willing to work side by side with these people and make common cause with them." This is the approach which Eugene R. Black recommends and which he calls "Development Diplomacy ";[29] it is the basic philosophy of the United States Peace Corps.

It has been recognized that the early phases of American and Western economic aid in the 1950's were more direct and the political strings attached were more obvious; that was in the days of the Aswan High Dam project.[30] But even the most subtle approach of more recent times and even in those numerous cases where no immediate political aims were pursued, the developing nations have been doubtful and suspicious. The search for ulterior motives is poisoning the atmosphere of international aid.

From the start, American development diplomacy faced certain difficulties. Most of the newly developing nations had been under colonial rule. The United States itself had emerged from such domination only relatively late in history; this, however, was forgotten since her closest allies are the colonial powers.

Observers of the foreign scene, such as Barbara Ward, [31] have pointed out that the old enemy - the colonial powers of Europe - has apparently been joined by the United States and the united Western world seemed to the emerging countries a renewal of the old menace. [32] Private capital that might be interested to invest in the underdeveloped economies is seen as a capitalistic threat to local welfare. Foreign government aid, whether in the form of grants or loans, is seen as a means of imperialistic policy that would endanger the country's newly won freedom and independence. The attempt made by American advisers in the course of their assistance program to participate in the planning stage, to ensure the effectiveness of the individual projects and the efficiency of their implementation is taken as proof of the intent to intervene in the affairs of the developing country.

Such suspicions and misgivings are not surprising. Due to the fundamental difference in the historic spiritual heritage of the developed and the new countries and the tremendous gap in their social and economic development, a common meeting ground does not seem to exist. An area of understanding might have been created through a slow process of getting acquainted and of common venture. The West, outgoing and optimistic and extending a helping hand in the spirit of friendship - whatever its motivating hopes and expectations - might, after a period of trial, have been accepted by the developing nations as a teacher and possibly as a partner in the period of growth. The policies of the Soviet bloc interrupted this development.

It has been in the interest of Soviet diplomacy to emphasize the fact that all American public and private aid is given with the intention of spreading American influence all over the world in the spirit of colonialism and imperialism, and these suggestions find willing reception in many new nations. The Communist bloc is in a position to offer proof that its own economic aid is quite free of such considerations; it is ready to support any programs sug-

gested by the underdeveloped nations themselves, without
forcing on their governments their own opinion as to the
wisdom of such enterprises. As has been stated in a study
on "Ruble Diplomacy", [33] the Communist countries

> refrain studiously from interfering with the in-
> vestment plans of the economically less devel-
> oped countries. They do not raise the question
> whether a steel mill here or a pharmaceutical
> factory there is what is most needed. In fact,
> they often seem to prefer the financing of pro-
> jects which have a high visibility - an oil refin-
> ery or railroad or pavements for the streets
> of Kabul - which have strong appeal to local go-
> vernments and populations and will stand as
> monuments to Communist helpfulness. [34]

Such meetings of the minds between economic advisers and local governments give Soviet influence effectiveness and emphasize an understanding between the Communist bloc and the developing countries.
       While any struggle that the United States or any other
Western power may have had to experience in the past before reaching the present stage of freedom and affluence
is of no topical interest, the successful rise of the Soviet
system still lives in people's memory. Although not an
underdeveloped country, it still belongs in the world of
the have-not nations. [35] This bond seems even stronger due
to the fact that the needs of the Soviet economy, as far as
agricultural and other prime commodities are concerned,
complement those of some underdeveloped countries and
permit an economic exchange that is of advantage to both
parties.
       This assistance, made palatable by a community of
interests, is the more attractive since it does not seem to
ask for any immediate political return. Soviet philosophy,
built on Marxist doctrine, is confident of the spread of
Communism, as, on the one hand, the spirit of trust and
friendship is being built up and, on the other hand, an effort is made to expose the United States policy as capitalistic exploitation of underdeveloped countries.
       There are certain built-in advantages that help the
U.S.S.R. in its relations with the new nations and that are
lacking in the case of the United States. John G. Stoes-

singer summarizes them as follows:

> It /the U.S.S.R. 7 could come to the nations
> that had just emerged from colonialism as the
> main protagonist of national self-determina-
> tion; to the colored peoples of the world it could
> come as a partly Asian nation; in countries
> where the merchant had long been an object of
> contempt, it could emphasize its hostility to
> capitalism; to fledgling agricultural states
> yearning for modern industrial economies it
> could present itself as the nation that had launched
> the interplanetary age; and lastly, it could ex-
> ploit its theory of the "inevitability" of Commu-
> nist victory by persuading the peoples of the
> new nations that by following the precepts of
> Marxism-Leninism they would have history on
> their side and could make the leap to progress
> almost through an act of faith. [36]

After the changes which Stalin's death had brought
about, the Soviet Union made the most of these possibilities. "Since 1953 nearly every underdeveloped country has
been approached by the Soviet Union, with a proposition
to expand trade or with a credit offer. Naturally, it has
been the neutralist group which has received the greatest
attention and some have developed significant ties to the
Soviet bloc. But even Western-oriented countries . . .
have expanded their economic contacts with the Soviet Union."[37]

While Soviet diplomacy has been able to minimize
the effect of American aid by keeping underdeveloped countries alert to the dangers of imperialism and capitalism,
the spectacle of two great powers competing with each other in the field of aid has not been lost on the new nations.
They are becoming aware of their own role in the world
and they have started to recognize that the U.S.S.R. and
the other Communist countries, too, have more in mind
than granting aid selflessly.

The emerging nations may at times be tempted to
benefit from the competition between free enterprise and
centrally planned economies and to accept help from both
sides. If this is done within the framework of a national
economic plan, such a policy may be sound. An analysis

of the assistance that can be offered by the United States
and by the Communist bloc has shown that the number of
economic instruments at the disposal of the Communist
countries is greater than that of the West, which can result
in more precision when reaching for a set of goals; on the
other hand, the instruments which the West uses are, though
less numerous, more efficient. As Jan Tinbergen puts
it: "In plain terms, Western economies may more easily
get out of control. They may, and generally do, reveal
instances of individual interest being served in opposition
to community interests and of very unequal income distribution, partly as a consequence of private ownership of
the means of production."[38] An optimum combination of
these factors can bring results to a developing economy
which are superior to those obtained by United States or
U.S.S.R. aid alone.

As the developing nations mature and come to appreciate their equal status in the community of sovereign nations, they start to reappraise their role in the cold war.
They realize that their economic integration cannot be
effected entirely through bilateral agreements with East
and West; and that foreign influence on their political, economic and social development can be avoided only if their
economic aims are discussed, and their economic problems
are approached in agreement both with other developing nations and with the developed countries in a spirit of cooperation within the framework of international organization.

4 INTERNATIONAL
MACHINERY REGULATING
ECONOMIC RELATIONS
BETWEEN DEVELOPED
AND DEVELOPING
NATIONS

1. EFFORTS PRIOR TO THE CONFERENCE

When representatives of various countries meet,
primary issues are war and peace and these have traditionally been the main topics of international conferences.

A step from the national to the international level
has also been taken to solve problems of internal governmental concern which affected a number of countries in
some way, and this accounts for the formation of functional agencies during the 19th century. At that time, economic relations were not considered the concern of governments. The economic life of a nation, as long as it
moved within the legal system, was the private affair of
its citizens, and its regulation was beyond the scope of
national or international interference. Bilateral agreements and conventions concerning trade were designed
to support that trend.

The League Covenant was in keeping with the tradition of economic laissez faire, although in the meantime
the underlying philosophy had changed in many countries.
Economic cooperation was not among the aims specified
in the League Covenant. Its only reference to trade was
the assurance that "the members of the League will make
provisions to secure and maintain equitable treatment for
the commerce of all members." (Article 23 (e)).

Nevertheless, some economic agencies were included in the organizational framework of the League.

The Economic and Financial Organization, originating in two previous commissions, [1] functioned on the basis
of the League's program to "promote international cooperation" and was staffed by experts. Its record was not
considered successful. The Organization called a series
of conferences, most of them connected with trade, tar-

iffs and exchange controls. Even before the establishment of the Organization, the League, in 1920, had a Conference in Brussels which dealt with worldwide financial and exchange crises. The eighty-six delegates to this Conference from thirty-nine countries attended as experts, rather than as spokesmen for the official policy of their countries, a practice which was generally adopted by the League for its technical organizations. Several international bodies, such as the International Labor Organization, were also represented in Brussels.

The largest and most important of the conferences held by the Economic and Financial Organization of the League were the Economic World Conference of 1927 in Geneva and the International Monetary and Economic Conference of 1933 in London, which aroused great hopes but did not lead to practical results.

The lack of success of economic organizations has been ascribed by some observers to the fact that the League was not "endowed with vast and readily mobilized resources."[2] Others contended that the experts who conducted the conferences did not have sufficient contact with national policy-makers and national problems in their own countries.[3] It has also been pointed out that the "mistaken policies of the nations which disregarded the interests of the other nations in the hope of benefiting themselves"[4] prevented the achievement of international collaboration, especially "if great trading powers all give priority to domestic considerations or operate on different sets of priorities when domestic and international policies come into conflict."[5] Other causes mentioned for lack of success were that a number of interested countries whose cooperation was essential were not members of the League for political reasons, notably the United States, and therefore did not come within its scope.[6]

In spite of the urgent need for international action, created by such developments as the worldwide depression of the 1930's, the Economic and Financial Organization of the League confined its work at that time to research and statistical studies.

One aspect of economic conditions on an international level eventually received the attention of the League although, by that time, it was too late for practical results. The Bruce Report, presented by a committee set up by the Council of the League in 1939 under the presidency of former Australian Prime Minister S.M. Bruce, stressed the importance of raising the standard of living throughout the world and of establishing an agency within the League for this purpose which would be both effective and representative.

Some of the functional organizations which were formed before World War I and shortly after, affected economic affairs, although not all of them were primarily designed for this purpose. Among these were the international river commissions, and such specialized agencies as the International Telegraph Union (May,1865), the Universal Postal Union (October,1874), all of which benefited economic relations between nations. The International Labor Organization, created at the close of World War I, in April, 1919, to improve conditions of labor throughout the world and to encourage cooperation between labor and management for increased production and productivity, had an impact on national economies and undertook the obligation to encourage the raising of living standards and full employment. The League did not prove successful in coordinating these various agencies. However, it provided a central focus for their activities, and it made its own contribution to mobilizing credits and loans to meet the emergency problems of individual countries and by collecting and publishing production statistics.

Independent of the League, a number of organizations were created during the war, to prepare the world for peace. They owed their existence to the realization that World War II and its aftermath would create serious problems for the victors as well as for the vanquished. Among these new organizations which served economic and social aims was the United Nations Relief and Rehabilitation Administration. Its program was set up in 1943 while the United Nations Organization was still in the blueprint stage. UNRRA, by definition, was intended to be temporary in duration and use. However, some of the principles established during its existence were applied to subsequent emergency and relief operations, such as the guiding principle that international agencies should help people help themselves; the development of technical assistance; and the arrangement that neither import nor export taxes were to be imposed on relief supplies. Certain difficulties, typical for later international organizations, were also encountered, such as the reluctance of the U.S.S.R. to delegate

decisions to an international agency and its insistence on
the veto power. [7]

These elements of economic collaboration before,
during and immediately after the existence of the League
proved useful. Partly through a process of trial and error,
partly through the accomplishment of narrowly defined aims,
avenues of international economic cooperation were explored, and a modest machinery was devised for this purpose.

It is true that the economic problems which occupied
international organizations before and shortly after World
War II were quite different from those which claimed the
attention of the United Nations and the specialized agencies ten years later. The needs of war-torn Europe and
of the Asian countries were the main concern at that earlier date and the aid extended was truly international, involving the movement of relief supplies across national borders. Economic assistance to underdeveloped countries,
which followed later, was in most instances of a different
character; the predominantly international nature was lent
by the fact that the needs of many nations - virtually all
of the colonialized and some of the other underdeveloped
nations - were basically the same and called for action by
the rest of the world.

As a result of the experience gained during the inter-
war period and in the course of events which followed the
outbreak of World War II, it had become apparent that
economic upheaval and social dissatisfaction played a large
role in the causes of war and political unrest. Looking
back on World War I and the Treaty of Versailles, Field
Marshal Jan Christian Smuts expressed the newly found
insight: "The framers of the peace lived . . . in a political world and were dominated by a political outlook and
point of view. They thought political solutions would suf-
fice . . . It soon became evident that economic chaos and
the social unrest and suffering resulting from it were no
less fruitful sources of war than the ordinary forms of
aggression, so familiar to the political world. "[8] The Field
Marshal's address was given at the Sixth Plenary Meeting
of the United Nations Conference on International Organization, on May 6, 1945. It expressed not only the interest
of the founders of the new organization in international economic conditions, but also the source of that interest. The
foremost aim of the new agency was not inherently differ-

ent from that which inspired the Congress of Vienna and
the League of Nations. Its aims, too, were peace and security. What had changed was the approach to the solution
of the problem of preventing wars. It was realized that
"a great deal of international strife was rooted in poverty
and misery and that, therefore, the United Nations should
do its utmost to help raise standards of living and improve
economic conditions throughout the world, "[9] and this realization created new interest in economic conditions and the
need for their improvement. Adopting this new approach
to peaceful coexistence, the United Nations Organization
was able to continue some of the more promising avenues
which the League and a few other agencies had started.

In line with this approach, the U.N. Charter makes
it clear that its authors considered economic goals of great
importance. The preamble states their determination "to
promote social progress and better standards of life in
larger freedom", and for this end "to employ international
machinery for the promotion of the economic and social advancement of all peoples. " Chapter I enumerates among
the aims of international cooperation the efforts to solve
international problems of an economic character. Chapter
IX maps out the program envisaged, including the promotion of higher standards of living, full employment, conditions of economic and social progress and development,
and the solution of international economic problems - all
these measures as part of a larger program which considers social, health and related problems in the spirit of
freedom, without distinction as to race, sex, language
or religion. Article 60 of that chapter places the responsibility for implementation of this program on the Economic
and Social Council under the authority of the General Assembly.

The decision to create the Economic and Social Council as one of the major United Nations Organs, responsible for cooperation in the economic and social fields was
made at the Dumbarton Oaks Conference, in October, 1944,
and was based on the recommendations of the Bruce Commission of 1939. [10]

According to Article 61, the Economic and Social
Council was to consist of eighteen members of the United
Nations, elected by the General Assembly. Six members
of ECOSOC are elected each year for a term of three years;
each member has one representative. The permanent mem-

bers of the Security Council - the United States, the Soviet
Union, Britain, France and China - became permanent
members of ECOSOC as well, and in the rest of the U.N.
membership, the developed nations seemed slightly favored. As part of the move to reflect the growing importance of African nations in the United Nations, ECOSOC
adopted a Resolution on July 22, 1963, calling upon the
General Assembly to take steps for improving the representation in the Council. A Resolution of the Assembly[11]
in December, 1963, provided for a revision of the Charter
which would expand the Economic and Social Council membership from eighteen to twenty-seven, of which nine are
to be elected each year for three-year terms. "Seven of
the new members would come from Asian and African states,
one from Latin American states, and one from Western
European and other states." United Nations members are
expected to ratify this amendment by September 1, 1965.
The amendment will be an improvement over the attempt
made to permit participation of underdeveloped nations,
included in Article 69, which gave members of the United
Nations the possibility of taking part in deliberations that
concern them without giving them a vote.

   The economic activities of the United Nations system
have been described as a "crazy-quilt pattern of responsibility"[12] although constitutionally, it would appear that the
Economic and Social Council has "the sum total of economic
and social matters before it" when preparing the annual
report to the Assembly. ECOSOC is not an operational
agency, however. Its task consists to a great extent in the
coordination and organization of work performed through
commissions and through the specialized agencies, and there
has been duplication of effort and overlapping, despite continued streamlining and simplification.

   According to Article 68, ECOSOC shall set up commissions in economic, social and related areas. There
are eight functional commissions through which the Council works, as well as regional commissions: for Europe
(ECE); for Asia and the Far East (ECAFE); for Latin America (ECLA); and for Africa (ECA). It is the merit of this
functional and regional approach that each regional organization can study one particular aspect of economic problems
within its own setting, and that it can hope to devise arrangements which fit the particular character of the nation or
the group of nations involved. The reports submitted by

the regional commissions provide material which facilitates evaluation of available resources and of needs to be
filled. Moreover, it provides the nations of the area with
"a United Nations forum of their own. "[13]
    Another task which the Charter assigns to ECOSOC
is the coordination of the specialized agencies. Article
63 empowers the Council to enter into agreements with
them, to bring them into relationship with the United Nations, and to coordinate their activities.
    Under the provision, eleven specialized agencies
have been brought into the United Nations system. Some
of these, for instance the Universal Postal Union, the International Tele-Communication Union, the International
Civil Aviation Organization, the Inter-Maritime Consultative Organization, while contributing to better communications, are expected not only to lessen the danger of war
but also to facilitate international commerce, and they
are thus of marginal interest in the solution of international problems. This group has been called the "housekeeping" force, as distinct from the "idealistic" agencies, [14]
which seek to improve world conditions. Some agencies
in the latter group are directly engaged in the promotion
of economic cooperation with the economic development of
emerging nations.
    Since a survey of problems which developing nations
face revealed that lack of capital was of crucial importance, measures were needed to facilitate the investment
of capital for productive purposes by direct financing arrangements and by measures designed to attract foreign
capital. To this end, the International Bank for Reconstruction and Development, known as the World Bank, was
founded by an agreement reached by the United Monetary
Fund Financial Conference, held in Bretton Woods in July,
1944. The Bank has, through experts, investigated the
situation in countries which seemed in need of its assistance and, on that basis, has extended advice on planning
and on improvement possibilities. The first mission of
World Bank experts was sent to Colombia upon the request
of its government in 1949, and since then general surveys
and specialized studies have been undertaken in many developing countries. [15] These surveys have occasionally
met with the criticism that the collection of detailed data
at times led to prolonged preliminary investigations[16] and
that the programs recommended by the IBRD missions of-

ten fell short of what was needed to attain real development. [17] The Bank's main function, the granting of development loans, has been performed in line with commercial principles, which follow sound investment policies.
"The World Bank . . . resembles a commercial lending
institution more than an international source of low interest, long-term easy repayment loans."[18] This approach
is of greater assistance to developed than to developing
countries, and it was the reason why the U.S.S.R. declined
to join the Bank, disregarding the fact that two affiliates
of that institution, the International Finance Corporation
and the International Development Corporation, have adopted a "soft loan" policy.

The discussions and considerations which brought the
Bank into being also led to the creation of the International
Monetary Fund. Since it was hoped that many of the problems of developing areas would be solved by foreign investment, credit and trade, differences in foreign currencies
could be expected to pose serious problems. An institution which provides machinery for consultation and collaboration about international monetary arrangements with
the responsibility of making orderly exchange arrangements
and avoiding competitive exchange depreciations, would,
it was believed, facilitate the expansion and balanced growth
of international trade. These were the tasks assigned to
the Fund, which works in close cooperation with the Bank
and, like the Bank, does not include the U.S.S.R. among
its members.

The Fund is clearly designed to promote trade among
nations in financial respects. Removal of other barriers
to world trade was attempted on a global scale by the International Trade Organization, which the United States proposed in 1945. Fifty-six nations met in Havana in 1947 to
draw up a charter for a new United Nations specialized
agency. When ITO became a casualty of the cold war, which
prevented functional cooperation in Havana, twenty-three
nations from the Atlantic Community and Latin America met
in Geneva and drafted instead a General Agreement on Tariffs
and Trade (GATT), in 1947. A hundred and twenty sets
of bilateral negotiations, embracing forty-three thousand
items, were incorporated in the agreements, [19] and additional members joined in subsequent years.

GATT was created to take a position in the old con-
troversy between free trade and protection. Its policies

are based on the principle that tariffs should assume their traditional role as the main instrument of commercial policy. Although basically, free trade is desirable, protection becomes a necessity under certain conditions. GATT, therefore, was designed to assure protection for developing countries under certain conditions as follows: for certain countries, if they have an insufficient share of the world's income, and in cases where it is difficult or impossible to organize subsidies for industries which have not yet reached their optimum size; and for all countries in cases where it is impossible to finance measures designed to enhance the mobility of capital and labor in any other way. [20]

The immediate need for food in many areas during World War II led to the establishment of another specialized agency. An international conference on food and agriculture held at Hot Springs in May, 1943, dealt with the prospect of scarcity in war-torn areas and with the long-standing conditions of food shortages in certain underdeveloped countries. The problems studied covered a wide range of contributing factors and focused on the inequality of distribution and the fact that the lack of food was a serious handicap in the development of some nations, while the overabundance in certain commodities was a burden to others. The Food and Agriculture Organization, founded at this Hot Springs Conference, was expected to study this and related problems and to take such measures which would approach their solution.

Since its establishment, the FAO has become interested in nutritional levels through a better distribution of foods and through the improvement of agricultural production by introducing modern technology; to accomplish this objective, the work of all the other specialized agencies - directly, indirectly and even remotely involved in economic problems - is required. Article 58 of the Charter recognizes this fact. It calls on the Economic and Social Council to make recommendations for the coordination of the policies and activities of the specialized agencies, and Article 59 expresses the expectation that the Council initiate negotiations among the states concerned for the creation of new agencies required for its purposes.

Material aid through the provision of supplies, capital investment, loans and other assistance to developing nations cannot be expected to solve their problems except on

an emergency basis. Such aid might satisfy immediate
needs, but it would underline the difference between the have
and the have-not nations and perpetuate the dependence of
the underdeveloped countries on the developed governments.
Internal economic policies in developed countries changed
in the past decades to a great extent from the paternalis-
tic attitude of welfare and relief provided for the indigent
to the promotion of plans which give them the opportunity
to improve themselves. A similar approach was needed
in the international field. The League realized the necessity of instructing member nations through direct advice
and through technical experts, and it utilized the machinery of three of its organizations - the Organizations for
Economics and Finance, for Commerce and Transit, and
for Health - to embark in a program which it called "Technical Collaboration" or "Cooperation". UNRRA was one
of the first international organizations which helped the developing nations to help themselves.

A similar program was launched by the United Nations Organization as a result of a report submitted in 1948
by the Sub-Committee on Economic Development to the Economic and Employment Commission of ECOSOC. This report was focused on increased assistance for economic development, a topic which at that time was also considered
by the Second and the Fifth Committees of the U.N. General
Assembly. This set a procedure in motion which resulted
in the appropriation of funds by the General Assembly, enabling the Secretary General, in cooperation with the specialized agencies and upon the request of member governments, to arrange for the organization of international
teams of experts to advise governments on their economic
development programs, to provide means for the training
of experts and local technicians in underdeveloped countries, and facilities to assist governments in obtaining personnel, equipment and supplies, as well as other services
for the promotion of economic development.

This was the beginning of the United Nations activities in the field of technical assistance. The incentive to
expand the program came from the interest which the proposed Point Four of President Harry S. Truman's inaugur-
al program, announced in 1949, aroused throughout the
world. The President's proposal to extend assistance to
the underdeveloped nations by means of a cooperative enterprise in which all nations would work together through

the United Nations and its specialized agencies, elaborated
by the United States Delegation to the U.N., prompted
the Economic and Social Council to request the Secretary
General, in consultation with the specialized agencies, to
formulate a comprehensive plan for technical assistance.
This plan led ultimately to a Resolution on Technical Assistance which was unanimously accepted by the General
Assembly. A Technical Assistance Board and a Technical
Assistance Committee were created, a number of regional
and functional commissions were formed, and advisory
and operating missions have been sent to underdeveloped
countries.

     After a slow start and considerable difficulties in
the planning stages, this program was accelerated in 1952,
and improved by the creation of resident representatives
for each member nation who were made responsible for
coordinating the activities of the participants in the host
country. In 1953, the U.S.S.R. expressed the intention
of joining the West in the Expanded Technical Assistance
Program. Although there was much speculation about the
motives behind this move, it was assumed that the success of ETAP and its popularity with the developing countries prompted Moscow's decision. [21]

     The proposed establishment of still another agency
has been the subject of discussions among the U.N. members for a number of years, and these discussions have
particularly underlined the different points of view of the
United States and the U.S.S.R. in dealing with international organization. In 1951, a Special United Nations Fund
for Economic Development (SUNFED) was suggested by a
number of developing nations. This fund was intended to
provide investment capital in the form of grants-in-aid.
At the time, the U.S.S.R. had not yet become interested
in assistance to developing nations, while the United States
was too deeply involved in the Korean War to make international financial commitments. In 1953, the U.S.S.R. began to participate in assistance to developing nations, favored long-term loans over grants, and joined the new nations in a request for the creation of SUNFED as an independent lending authority within the United Nations system.
The continued opposition of the United States has been based
on the contention that a number of existing agencies already perform the task which SUNFED was supposed to
undertake, and that U.S. bilateral assistance already pre-

sents the maximum sum available for foreign aid. Since
Moscow in recent years has also seemed reluctant to provide additional funds for such a program, the SUNFED issue has lost its importance. [22]

Meanwhile, in 1959, the Special Fund was established
to support a program of sustained assistance in development research. Among the programs which have been conducted within the framework of the U.N. system, EPTA
and the Special Fund occupy a prominent place. Their
work was moving ahead smoothly in 1961 and 1962, even
while the United Nations itself faced serious financial difficulties because of the Congo situation and various political considerations. [23] EPTA increased in 1961 by more
than twenty-three per cent and in 1962 showed a further
rise. Advances have been made not only in the amounts
of funds made available but also in programming. With
reduced assistance to other areas, increasing resources
have been devoted to Africa, where the emergence of many
new states steadily created new problems. The operation
of the new International Development Association (IDA)
has enabled poorer economies to take advantage of loans
under favorable conditions.

Nevertheless, the total amount expended by the developed nations during a period of nearly twenty years in
money and in manpower has failed to bridge the gap between
the developed and the underdeveloped economies. International cooperation, as it has been practiced heretofore,
has not accomplished its aim. A study of the reasons for
this insufficiency pointed to one area of international relations which so far has not received enough attention. The
General Agreement on Tariffs and Trade has established
principles which benefited the developing countries to a
certain extent. But GATT did not go far enough, no attempt was made to study deeply the impact of trade policies of the developed countries on the developing economies
and no concerted effort was undertaken to use trade measures as an instrument. It was because of these deficiencies that a search was started for a new trade policy.

In 1962, eleven developing nations sponsored a Conference in which thirty-one additional developing nations
participated; while observers were sent by five developing countries, by the United Nations, and by a number of
specialized agencies, and by some regional groupings.
The "Conference on the Problems of Economic Develop-

ment" met in Cairo, and its agenda listed the following
items: Internal Problems facing the Developing Countries;
Promotion of Economic, Technical and Trade Cooperation
and Development of Transportation among Developing
Countries; Economic Development and Trade between the
Developing and Developed Countries; and Economic and
Technical Assistance to the Developing Countries. [24] The
Conference, culminating in the Cairo Declaration, was
considered highly successful and of great significance for
international cooperation among developing countries. However, the very fact that it was undertaken by developing
countries limited its importance. Attempts to solve trade
and development problems by developing countries alone
had as little chance to show real results as the same efforts expanded by developed countries alone. The fusion
of both efforts, it was thought, might possibly lead to a
full measure of success.

2. THE PREPARATORY COMMITTEE OF THE CONFERENCE

On December 19, 1961, the General Assembly expressed its conviction that expansion of trade and increase
in foreign exchange income as a result of growth in volume
and value of exports offered the most rapid method of aiding the development of new nations; that the economic policies of regional and subregional economic groupings should
avoid the introduction and should facilitate the elimination
of obstacles and restrictions which might hamper the necessary expansion of the trade of the developing countries or
discourage the indispensable growth of their economies.
The resolution adopted on this subject[25] went on to enumer-
ate some of the practices and policies which are detriment-
al to the growth of international trade; it reaffirmed the duty
of the more highly industrialized countries to cooperate in
accelerating the economic development of the developing
and underdeveloped countries; it reminded the nations participating that a more rapid rate of economic growth is in
the interest of all countries; and it recognized the responsibility of the United Nations and of the other international bodies to provide ways and means for finding and furthering effective solutions to achieve this purpose.

After discussing in greater detail the steps necessary to implement these policies, and calling for the cooperation of member nations and international agencies, the resolution requested the Secretary General to consult governments of U.N. members and members of the specialized agencies to ascertain their view on the advisability of holding an international conference on international trade problems, with special reference to primary commodity markets and, if such a conference was deemed advisable, the topics that might be considered for a provisional agenda.

In a resolution of the same day, [26] the current decade was designated as the "United Nations Development Decade" in which member states and their peoples are expected to intensify their efforts to mobilize and to sustain support for the measures required on the part of both developed and developing countries, in order to accelerate progress toward self-sustaining growth of the economies of individual nations.

The Economic and Social Council recalled these resolutions in its Plenary Meeting of August 3, 1962, gave attention to the current economic world situation and its problems and to the solution pursued by the General Agreement on Tariffs and Trade, and referred to the replies of many governments of member states to the questionnaire of the Secretary General on the desirability of convening an international conference, as suggested by the General Assembly. Acting on these instructions, ECOSOC decided to convene a United Nations Conference on Trade and Development, and to convene, by early spring 1963, a Preparatory Committee, and requested the Secretary General, with the assistance of other international agencies, to prepare for consideration by the Preparatory Committee, appropriate documentation and proposals for such a conference. [27]

Expert representatives, designated by governments which are represented on the Economic and Social Council, met as the Preparatory Committee to draw up a provisional agenda for the Conference and to outline a substantial program of research to be undertaken by the Secretariat. The nations represented by delegates were Argentina, Australia, Austria, Brazil, Canada, Colombia, Czechoslovakia, Denmark, San Salvador, Ethiopia, France, Italy, Japan, Jordan, Lebanon, Madagascar, New Zealand, Nigeria, Pakistan, Peru, Poland, Senegal, Tunisia, Union of Soviet Socialist Republics, United Arab Republic, United

Kingdom of Great Britain and Northern Ireland, United
States of America, Uruguay and Yugoslavia. There were
also a number of observers from non-member governments,
as well as representatives of specialized agencies and non-
governmental organizations.

At the first session, held from January 22 to February 5, 1963, the participating delegations concurred on
basic issues. They generally agreed that there was a functional relationship between trade and economic development
and that international trade was an integral part of national development plans and programs, as well as closely related to other national and international policies. This
broader approach to the problem of international trade guided the discussion on the ways and means of improving cooperation[28] as well as on the implementation of trade policies.

After twenty-two meetings, the groundwork was laid
for the proposed conference. The agenda adopted stated
and defined the objectives of the conference by summariz-
ing them under seven main headings. [29]

I.   Expansion of International Trade and its Significance
     for Economic Development
     This first item explored the ultimate significance on
the economies of underdeveloped nations of trade between
countries on the same or on different economic levels of
development, operating under the same or under different
economic and social systems. The question thus posed
was obviously broad and general, and any possible answers had to indicate the basic needs of developing countries as part of their over-all growth. The agenda suggested a review of existing trends, a study of the impact which
these trends had on the underdeveloped economies as well
as problems arising out of the existing situation, and the
formulation of principles which might be conducive to the
improvement of trade relations.

II. International Commodity Problems
     The second topic expressed the Committee's recogni-
tion of the fact that primary commodities have been and are
expected to remain for some time to come the most important resource available to developing nations. It was agreed
that there was need for a survey of the national and world
demand for primary commodities; the possibilities of mini-

mizing market fluctuations and of stabilizing the income
from such commodities; and of means to promote trade
among developing countries themselves - not only between
them and developed countries.

III.   Trade in Manufactures and Semi-Manufactures
        The Committee concerned itself here with the advance
of industrialization.   Only if finished and semi-finished
goods, produced in the developing economies, find a market
in the developed countries, can the rate of industrialization
of the developing countries be maintained or accelerated.
Tariffs and quantitative restrictions imposed on such goods
will lead to the accumulation of a stockpile in developing
economies and not only cause a slowdown in their production, but ultimately lead to a standstill of their economies.
The study was also designed to explore the possibilities of
increased trade of finished and semi-finished goods among
developing countries.

IV.   Improvement of the Invisible Trade of the Developing
      Countries
        Since the balance of payments is not only influenced
by the movement of goods across boundaries but also by
services, mainly in connection with tourist trade, transportation and insurance costs, and servicing of the public
debt, an improvement in the service account was recommended and studied.

V.   Implications of Regional Economic Groupings
        In the opinion of the Preparatory Committee, the
trade expansion of developing countries was influenced in
different ways and in different degrees by regional groupings of two kinds: by those of developing countries, and
by others in which developed countries participated.   It
was agreed that the study of the impact which the two types
of organizations had on the underdeveloped countries should
be conducted separately.

VI.   Financing for an Expansion of International Trade
        Since financing of foreign trade and the acquisition
of capital equipment constituted one of the major problems
which underdeveloped countries encountered in their en-
deavors to expand their economies, a mechanism for establishing medium and long-term credit was essential.   A

study of the possibilities for establishing such a mechanism
was the subject of Item VI. One section of the chapter also referred to programs of technical assistance which
should be coordinated with trade and aid policies. This,
in the view of some delegates, was a reference to the training of national technical personnel.

VII. Institutional Arrangements, Methods and Machinery
      to Implement Measures Relating to the Expansion of
      International Trade
      This section called for a reappraisal of the effective-
ness of existing international bodies in the field of international trade, and for the elimination of overlapping and
duplication by coordination or consolidation of the activities of such bodies. The two paragraphs are taken verba-
tim from the General Assembly Resolution 1785 that initiated the Conference. Definite recommendations and decisions were expected to crystallize after a full discussion
on all related problems in the course of the Conference.

      It was envisaged that a Final Act would conclude the
agenda of the Conference.

      The provisional agenda was drawn up and incorporat-
ed in a Report in the First Session of the Preparatory Committee, submitted to the Economic and Social Council. The
Council resolved[30] that the Second Session of the Preparatory Committee should meet for a period of six weeks beginning on May 21, 1963. This session actually ended on
June 29, 1963.
      The number of participants was increased for the se-
cond and third sessions by representatives of two member
states from Asia and the Far East - Malaya and Indonesia;[31]
this was a step designed to secure an appropriate balance
of representation in the Committee.
      During its second session, the Preparatory Committee
studied the material that had been prepared on the objectives of the Conference by the Secretariat, by member governments, and by regional economic commissions, specialized agencies and the Commission on International Commodity Trade. It also examined its own tentative agenda,
drawn up at its first session, and the action taken by the
Economic and Social Council on its fifty-fifth session, to
which it had been submitted.

Meanwhile, another document had been prepared and made available to the Preparatory Committee at its second session. On August 3, 1962, [32] the Economic and Social Council, recognizing the importance of an improved trade position of developing countries for the success of the United Nations Development Decade, requested the Secretary General to appoint a small group of highly qualified experts with practical experience to prepare a report which had the following aims: to survey and evaluate the activities of various international organizations on commodity problems and on other trade problems of particular importance to the developing countries, and to propose any additional activities that would be desirable as well as the means of making them effective.

The authors of the report, twelve experts in the field who acted in their personal capacity, met during the period February 18 to March 8, 1963, in New York, and from May 6 to May 20 in Geneva. In their letter of transmittal to the Secretary General, they pointed out that the members of their group were divided both in their assessment of the existing situation and on their recommendations as to the steps which might be taken to enable the international organizations to deal more effectively with trade problems, and that these divergent opinions were expressed in the document. In particular, four different proposals were presented for the institutional arrangement which was one of the objectives of this study. One proposal called for the establishment of a new international trade organization; another favored some modification in the machinery of the Economic and Social Council and the General Assembly; the third proposed the strengthening of the General Agreement on Tariffs and Trade; and the fourth suggested the creation of a permanent forum for United Nations member nations. A preliminary version of the experts' report was submitted to the Preparatory Committee.

In a number of sub-committees set up by the Preparatory Committee, the seven main issues were further investigated, a definitive draft of the preliminary agenda was prepared and the necessary documentation was provided.

The report of the second session of the Preparatory Committee was presented to the Economic and Social Council at its thirty-sixth session. The Council then resolved[33] that the United Nations Conference should be held in Geneva between March 23 and June 15, 1964.

At the third session of the Preparatory Committee which opened on February 3, 1964, additional reports by the Secretary General and by some member nations were received. However, the principal topics of discussions were housekeeping matters and technical, procedural and administrative measures to be taken in preparation for the Conference meetings.

This set of various studies and reports completed the task of the Preparatory Committee. Dr. Raul Prebisch, of Argentina, the Secretary General of the United Nations Conference on Trade and Development, paid tribute to the "extensive and creative labors of the Preparatory Committee of the Conference."[34]

An evaluation of the work done by the Preparatory Committee must take into consideration the conditions under which it functioned. When the Economic and Social Council resolved to set up a Preparatory Committee, the frame of reference for the Committee had been already established. A decision had been reached to call a Conference on Trade and Development, and the basic aims of that Conference had been determined. It was felt to be "vital for the world community to create an international trade environment that would facilitate the growth of developing countries and not thwart it, " and, as Secretary General U Thant further explained, this was the basic aim of the Conference.[35] It was therefore beyond the scope of the Preparatory Committee to determine whether or not international trade was actually the single most important policy through which development could be promoted. The expert delegates who convened for the three sessions were committed to the approach taken by the General Assembly and the Economic and Social Council. Their main task consisted in the preparation of an agenda which would give the Conference the opportunity of discussing all those aspects of international trade regarded as essential for international development.

To this end, the Preparatory Committee had to analyze the problems of international trade and to select those which had bearing on development. Moreover, it had to organize the relevant issues in the proper order which would facilitate discussion of each question, sufficiently introduced and prepared, and in turn to prepare the background for the next point. All this work had to be done

on the basis of recommendations made by member states
and international organizations in a spirit of compromise
and conciliation. Only if the have and the have-not nations,
the West, the Communist bloc and the uncommitted governments were ready to accept the program, could there be
any hope for a fruitful conference. These are the conditions in terms of which the success of the Preparatory Committee has to be gauged.

The method by which the Preparatory Committee approached its delicate task was well suited to the accomplishment of its aims. The members of the Committee undertook an extensive study of material prepared on the subject matter. The documentation on which they based their
deliberations included more than a dozen reports prepared
by the Secretariat, which reviewed such topics as trends
of world trade; trade problems between developing countries and centrally planned economies, as well as between
countries at different stages of development; long-term
trends, expansion of market opportunities and financing.
It further included suggestions submitted by a large number
of governments, by regional commissions, by specialized
agencies and their commissions, by minutes of meetings
of ECOSOC, and by the report of the twelve experts appointed by the Secretary General.

This extensive documentation accomplished a number of purposes. It made it possible for the members of
the Preparatory Committee to become thoroughly acquainted with the principles and the thinking in the fields of trade
and development, and to familiarize themselves with the
treatment of related problems by existing international
and regional bodies. It also made them aware of measures
taken in the search for solutions, and of the limitations
which had been discovered in the course of this search.

Whether, on the basis of this study, the choice of
items for the agenda was judicious and whether the topics
had been selected and presented in the right order were to
become apparent during the Conference. The provisional
agenda, although not altogether binding, and subject to adjustment, was to determine the organization and the flow
of work during the conference sessions and, to a certain
extent, be responsible for the smoothness of procedure.

The documentation also gave members of the Preparatory Committee the opportunity to study the attitude of
member governments in connection with the discussions and

to consider the approach they would take as well as their
respective hopes and ambitions.

At the sessions of the Preparatory Committee, the
issues at stake were discussed and clarified. Although
the desirability of international action in the field of trade
had been generally understood and although it constituted
the element which united the otherwise divergent groups
in the U. N. membership, actual priorities depended on national needs. Immediate aims, long-term plans and the
vested interests of the individual countries prompted their
attitude to particular issues. Distrust of ultimate aims
and ulterior motives often produced opposition where opposition was least expected. This was illustrated at an
early stage in the preparation of the Conference, when
Moscow's readiness to participate aroused the suspicion
of the United States. Washington believed that the anta-
gonism of the U. S. S. R. to the General Agreement on Tariffs and Trade prompted Communist endorsement of a Conference on Trade and Development, and anticipated a further
fragmentation of efforts in behalf of international trade rather than a step toward the solution of existing problems.
This explains the reluctance of the United States to expect
constructive results from the Conference. Another source
of disagreement was due to the view of some developed nations that the developing nations themselves should assume
a greater share of responsibility for their own development.
The developed nations emphasized the role of domestic policies in developing economies, and called attention to the
need for structural reform.

These and other disagreements served to clarify the
areas of conflict without disrupting the sessions. A certain measure of agreement was reached through the com-
monly felt need to accomplish the immediate goal of solving some of the problems of developing countries, even
if other aims, specifically favored by some of these countries, had to be temporarily shelved. The Preparatory
Committee found that ". . . it was apparent that all delegations were determined to give the different agenda items
specific content, which would lead to the adoption of practical measures and to effective action for the benefit of
the developing countries."[36]

The most important accomplishment of the Preparatory Committee was the creation of this spirit of cooperation. For this atmosphere of conciliation facilitated the

drafting of the provisional agenda and encouraged hopes for a successful Conference.

1. THE PLENARY MEETINGS

The Opening Session

The Conference on Trade and Development was not meant to be "just another ordinary conference."[1] Every effort was made to lift that Conference out of the routine of international organizational life and to give it the character of a unique occasion.

The groundwork had been laid for over a year. In January, 1963, Dr. Raul Prebisch, the former Executive Secretary of ECLA, had been appointed Secretary General of the Conference. Heading a staff of international civil servants, he had started to provide the foundation for every aspect of the meetings. He, himself, had toured the world during previous months to gain first-hand impressions on the most recent developments in the economic field. The Preparatory Committee had studied the problems of trade and development and drawn up a provisional agenda, explained in detail and carefully documented, and it had devised rules and procedures that would ensure the smooth operation of the Conference machinery. The Secretary General of the Conference himself had prepared a report entitled, "Towards a New Trade Policy for Development", in which he had analyzed the needs of member nations in the economic field and had proposed certain measures of relief.

During the week preceding the formal opening, the various delegations met informally in Geneva to discuss the technical aspects of their participation.

The special character of the Conference was expressed not only by the elaborate advance preparations, but also by the number of nations which declared their interest in attending the Conference. One hundred and twenty countries sent representatives to Geneva.[2] Most of the governments delegated cabinet ministers to attend at least some of the meetings. With very few exceptions,

the world community thus showed its commitment to the idea
of international cooperation and its trust in international
organization.

On March 23, 1964, at the Palais des Nations in Geneva, some two thousand delegates and observers assembled
for the formal opening of the Conference. After an introduction by Dr. Raul Prebisch, the President of the Swiss
Confederation, Ludwig von Moos, addressed the Assembly.
He was followed by Secretary General of the United Nations, U Thant, and, after a president had been elected,
by the President of the Conference, Dr. Abdel Moneim
El-Kaissouni, Vice-Premier for Financial and Economic
Affairs of the United Arab Republic.

The rest of the first meeting was devoted to technical matters, the adoption of procedural rules, the constitution of some committees and the election of officers.
In addition to a General Committee and a Credential Committee, five main committees were needed for dealing with
the five main issues contained in the Preparatory Committee's provisional agenda, which was adopted by the Plenary Meetings. These five committees were appointed at
the Plenary Meetings. The chairmen of these committees, together with the President, the Vice-Presidents and
the Rapporteur of the Conference constituted the General
Committee.

The First Plenary Meeting of the Conference opened
the sessions formally; it also set the mood of the Conference. The large attendance, impressive for delegates and
observers, actually represented a potential threat to effectiveness and efficiency. This danger was met by drawing a
great number of representatives into active participation.
The election of numerous officers also offered the opportunity of permitting representation of all parts of the world,
all types of economic and social order, and all stages of
development. Twenty-seven vice-presidents were elected
according to regional groupings; eight from Western Europe, the United States and Canada; four from Eastern European countries; ten from African and Asian nations; and
five from Latin America. The composition of the Credential Committee followed the same concept.

The mood of the Conference was also determined by
the three opening speeches. It was Secretary General U
Thant who referred to the fundamental issue that had giv-
en rise to the need for the Conference: the "dilemma of

our times" which he identified as the fact that political
emancipation is not accompanied by a desirable rate of
economic progress. He, as well as the President of the
Swiss Confederation, saw a new "international division
of labor"[3] as one of the main instruments for the achievement of global economic development.

The growing awareness of a common obligation to
humanity and of a community of interest and economic interdependence was also stressed by the President of the
Conference, who described the ultimate aim of the meetings as the effort to assist in "creating an enduring part-
nership among the nations of the world." He called for
the political will and concerted action toward a bold new
policy of international cooperation. [4]

The Debate

On March 24, 1964, at the Third Plenary Meeting
of the Conference, Secretary General Dr. Prebisch introduced the General Debate with a statement which summed
up the key issue; the main efforts to accelerate the economic development of the developing countries had to be
made by their own governments. These efforts would find
expression in their exports. It was the intention of the
Conference to assist the developing countries to achieve
this aim by helping them to control economic forces instead
of being dominated by them.

Analyzing the economic areas which needed improvement, he drew special attention to the fact that the terms
of trade had to be considered, and that the beneficial effect of foreign aid granted to developing countries was nullified by terms of trade with developed countries which did
not consider the needs of developing economies. Repeat-
ing the call for "international cooperation" which had been
sounded during the First Plenary Session, he urged that
this approval be translated into quantitative targets cover-
ing exports of both primary and industrial goods from the
developing nations, and that such targets be set by developed free enterprise countries as well as by socialist
economies. He thought it wise to refrain from trying to
achieve too much, and termed the measures he had suggested as minimum requirements. He summed up the measures in six points:

1. to improve access to the world's markets for

the primary goods of developing countries with
quantitative targets to be reached within a certain number of years;
2. to improve and stabilize the purchasing power
of developing countries, derived from their exports either through commodity agreements or
compensatory financing, both linked to easier
access markets;
3. to promote the entry of manufactures and semi-
manufactures from developing into developed
countries;
4. to encourage and rationalize the policy of import substitution through regional groupings;
5. to encourage trade with socialist countries;
6. to decrease the burden of expenses for developing countries resulting from insurance, trans-
port and other disbursements of invisible trade.[5]

These points had been more fully explored in the previously published report of the Secretary General. They
now served as a basis for further discussion.

The Debate which followed during twenty-one Plenary
Meetings of the Conference, from March 24 to April 8,
1964, gave the participating nations the possibility to make
their position clear in a world forum, to air their grievan-
ces and to publicize their views, to explain and justify
their approach and to suggest solutions for their problems.

The work of the Preparatory Committee, the report
presented by the Secretary General of the Conference, and
the addresses which opened the Plenary Sessions should
have made it abundantly clear that the spirit of the Conference was one of international cooperation, aimed at bridg-
ing the gap between developed and developing economies,
and that all sovereign nations which participated met at
an equal basis and had a common aim. Paul Martin, Minister of External Affairs of Canada, found the right expression when he stated that the Conference had been called
in order to take a step forward in meeting the "revolution
of rising expectations" on which the people of the developing countries were embarked. [6]

Nevertheless, the speeches prepared for the Debate
by some representatives indicated that their countries were
still apprehensive about their role in the world. One delegate deemed it necessary to mention that his country was
not ashamed of being underdeveloped, as this was not due

to any fault of its own;[7] another felt it important to stress
that the developing countries had not come to stretch out
their hands for alms;[8] while a third wished that the advanced industrialized nations would realize that "the developing nations are not invoking pity, nor are they ask-
ing for charity."[9]

That this self-conscious attitude was outdated became
even more clear during the Debate. In speech after speech
the representatives of the participating states did their utmost to explain to their peers what, in their opinion, was
wrong with the present system of trade relations and what
they considered prime issues for the consideration of the
Conference.

Although each delegation spoke for its own government and for its own economy, the indications of certain
kinships among nations became discernible. As could
be expected, there were similarities in the approach of
developing countries on the one hand, and of industrialized countries on the other.[10] Major stress was placed
on some issues by countries which had arrived at similar
stages of development.[11] There were also unmistakable
signs of the East-West division, although the infusion of
cold war issues was deplored. Delegates who regretted
the absence of representatives from the People's Republic of China, the People's Democratic Republic of Korea,
the Democratic Republic of Viet Nam and the German Democratic Republic, as a rule also declared their determination to disregard the representatives of the Union of South
Africa and of Portugal. They ascribed the economic difficulties of developing countries to the continuing threat
of new colonialism and to the discriminatory practices of
capitalist economies.[12] These were the countries which
found the General Agreement on Tariffs and Trade of no
value for the regulation of tariffs and trade, and called for
a new trade organization under the auspices of the United
Nations.

This flat indictment of GATT was not shared by nations outside the Soviet bloc and its sympathizers.[13] The
International Chamber of Commerce staunchly defended
GATT without reservation.[14] Virtually all other nations
agreed that some reorganization of GATT was essential,
since in its present form it was not equipped to promote
trade relations between developed and developing countries. The representative of South Africa expressed the

majority view when he stressed the wealth of experience
embodied in GATT with regard to all aspects of international trade, and asked for improvements in such areas
as preferential arrangements among regional groupings,
industrial development and questions of reciprocity where
developing countries were concerned. [15]

Although a proliferation of international machinery
was not considered desirable and the reform of GATT was
preferred, there was widespread realization that the improvement of trade relations was a continuous process
which had to be maintained by special efforts. This explains
why a large number of nations favored permanent machinery with a standing conference, to forestall problems. The
delegations which specifically mentioned this requirement
in the Debate, came from different political groups and
were at different stages of development. [16]

Another proposal, originating in the Soviet bloc, also
found fairly wide support. The U.S.S.R. suggested a study
of the effect that general disarmament would have on the
economy of developing nations. The possibilities of this
approach appealed not only to the Communist states and
to their sympathizers, but also to nations which are uncommitted and to some which are Western-oriented. [17]

One of the most fundamental choices which faces nations in their efforts to achieve economic goals is whether
they wish to join other nations in the same area of the world
which are supposedly in a similar economic situation. The
majority of nations whose representatives discussed this
matter in the Conference Debates were in favor of regional
arrangements. Only a few were concerned with the possibility that global cooperation and the development of international trade might suffer from regional preoccupation, and with the fear that groupings of developed nations
might threaten the economic opportunities of developing
economies.

Discussion of this nature indicated that the attitude
of a given nation toward a particular problem, as might
be expected, is likely to be determined by its own experience and by the anticipated effects of a given measure on
its economy. This became especially apparent when some
participants brought up specific problems such as those
arising from the increasing use of synthetics and substitutes. [19]

Other instances which showed how a country's own

point of view and experience led to recommendations made
for the benefit of all countries were the advice of the Swiss
delegate to the developing countries to explore at an early
stage the possibilities of specialization in industry;[20] the
comment made by the Austrian representative that economic changes depended on ideological values as much as on
material conditions;[21] and the view developed by the representative of the United States which expressed the conviction that the achievement and maintenance of full employment and of a high rate of economic growth in industrial
countries was the first prerequisite for the improvement
of conditions in developing countries.[22] This view was
bitterly opposed by the delegate from Jamaica.[23] The
Philippines stressed the promotion of tourist trade as a
main problem for some developing countries;[24] while the
Republic of Viet Nam drew attention to the fact that mono-
polistic tendencies posed a threat not only to domestic economies but were becoming prevalent in international commerce, and especially in the fields of insurance and shipping.[25]

Such differences of opinion and special concerns expressed by a number of states only served to underline the
consensus of opinion which existed about the basic aims of
the Conference, as interpreted by the Secretary General.

General emphasis was placed on the problems of basic commodities and on manufactured and semi-manufac-
tured goods produced in developing countries; on the need
to ensure an expanded and more stable market at a fair
price level for basic commodities; on the need for opening up new markets for infant industries.

Some countries felt concern over the tendency to
look for a set of rules which would be established to guide
trade relations. Belgium warned against adopting sweep-
ing, all-embracing measures and recommended a commodi-
ty-by-commodity approach.[26] The representative of the
United Kingdom urged that a pragmatic approach be adopted to meet the differing needs of developing countries without making the attempt to find rules of permanent and universal application.[27]

For weeks, the speeches of the delegates - predict-
able for the insider, but barely distinguishable one from
another for the outsider - followed each other. After sixteen sessions, the representative from the Republic of
Niger warned that the Conference must not degenerate into

a dialogue, but should serve as a meeting place which would give each participant the full realization of its national potential. [28] This warning might have been more appropriate had the Plenary Meetings of the Conference been its main instrument. But while the sessions held at the Palais des Nations, in the full glare of publicity, created the image of the Conference on Trade and Development for the world, and were the focus of public attention, the actual work was done elsewhere. The addresses of high officials, the messages sent by heads of state, the speeches and statements by delegates provided the atmosphere of goodwill, in which international cooperation could be achieved. The temper of the Plenary Meetings confirmed the confidence of the world - of both the rich nations and the poor, of the Soviet bloc, the West and the uncommitted - in the United Nations system. This was the most significant aspect of the discussions.

2. THE COMMITTEES AT WORK

The provisional agenda, drawn up by the Preparatory Committee, contained five major issues which were intended to cover the area of trade and development. The First Plenary Meeting approved this provisional agenda.

The statements made by the delegates during the Debate dealt in the main with general principles and policies. Although it was possible to discern the stand which each country took in reference to the basic questions involved, details were seldom discussed. The Plenary Meetings were not, and were not meant to be, working sessions.

For an extensive study of the issues, five committees were set up. Here, problems were reviewed; the differences in opinion were discovered and analyzed; proposals were worked out and solutions suggested. The reports these committees rendered differed in content and in appearance, and reflected the different working methods adopted. Scrutiny of the work performed by the committees reveals the main problems of the Conference, and the extent to which active cooperation on the international level contributed to proposed solutions.

The First Committee

One of the subjects which the Preparatory Committee had designated for study was that of "International Commodity Problems", which was concerned with primary commodities, particularly with long-term trends and prospects for procedures; a program of measures and action for the removal of all kinds of obstacles and discriminatory practices, the expansion of market opportunities, increases in consumption and imports in developed countries; the promotion of trade among developing countries; the stabilization of markets at equitable and remunerative prices; and compensatory financing. [29]

A number of countries submitted to the First Committee for its consideration specific proposals, connected with these issues.

In seventeen meetings, with B. Greenspun of Argentina for Chairman, C. H. G. Amartunga of Ceylon for Vice-Chairman, and G. S. Magombe of the United Republic of Tanganyika and Zanzibar for Rapporteur, these problems were discussed. [30] Nineteen documents, partly contributed by the Secretary General of the Conference, partly by international agencies and by experts in the field, aided the Committee in the search for workable solutions.

In the course of these discussions, it appeared that there was one problem which, although not included in the tentative listing of important items, was a cause for great concern for many nations. This was the effect of synthetics and of other substitutes on trade, particularly with reference to primary products exported wholly or mainly from the developing countries. The rapid growth in the production of synthetics posed a problem in three ways: 1. by reducing the demand for the natural material, 2. by increasing price competition, thus exerting a downward pressure on the price of the natural material, 3. by introducing a special risk into long-term investments in the production of the natural product.

The Committee decided to set up a task force "Working Party 1 on Synthetics and Substitutes", which would study the problem and submit its recommendations. The Working Party consisted of thirteen members, representing a cross section of nations, and was joined by a consultant from the Food and Agriculture Organization. In the course of six meetings, this problem was reviewed, and a report was issued.

First, the nature of the problem was fully explored:

its causes, its effect, and the prognosis for its future development. Then, the need for remedial action was stressed.
Finally, recommendations were made concerning measures
which could be adopted by the developing countries, such
as an increase in the efficiency of production and in the
quality of the product; measures which would require cooperation between developed and developing countries, such
as the exchange of statistical information and international
investment planning and coordination; and measures which
would have to be taken by the industrialized countries, such
as the removal of tariff barriers and compensatory financing. In conclusion, it was recommended that the subject
should be kept under continued scrutiny by appropriate bodies within the United Nations system.

A summary of this report rendered by the Working
Party 1 was included in the report which the First Committee prepared on its total activity. To facilitate the
composition of that report, including proposals and recommendations, the First Committee appointed another
task force, the "Drafting Group, Working Party 2".

Another working party was set up by some developing countries within the First Committee, to conduct a
study of organization of commodity trade. Their recommendations, too, were incorporated into the report of the
First Committee.

In eighteen sessions, between May 12 and 29, 1964,
thirty-four delegates who were joined by observers from
some other countries met to review the draft reports prepared by the Rapporteur of the Committee, to discuss the
various aspects under consideration and to reach conclusions as to suggestions of possible solutions.

The report of the First Committee reveals[31] that
each item on the agenda was treated separately. First,
the issue was restated and expounded; objectives and principles were presented; background material and statistics
were used to analyze the present situation, to find the causes of shortcomings and difficulties and to predict future
development. In some instances, the details of discussions conducted during Committee meetings, were included.

One of the items on the agenda was, for instance,
the review of the long-term trends and prospects for primary commodity producers, including terms of trade. After searching for the root of the foreign trade difficulties
facing the developing countries and other countries highly

dependent on a narrow range of primary commodities, and after stating the causes for the adverse trends in the trade of the developing countries, the Committee summed up its findings as follows:

> The problem may, therefore, succinctly be stated thus: unless new policy measures in the field of trade, aid and finance provide additional resources for developing countries in the amount required, and a measure of stabilization be brought about in their export earnings at remunerative and equitable levels, it will be exceedingly difficult for developing countries to attain the target rate of growth set by the United Nations Development Decade.

This, in turn, led to the conclusion that

> measures should be drawn up and implemented with the end in view that export earnings from trade in primary commodities should make a maximum contribution to the solution of the trade and development problems of the developing countries.

A program of such measures and action was worked out on that basis.

Then, recommendations were made. These recommendations went into great detail, setting forth steps for implementation, for action of various types to be taken by developed countries as well as by underdeveloped countries, and by international organizations, for promotional methods and work programs. In cases where individual nations or groups of states objected to the steps and measures outlined in this recommendation, the statements made by dissenting delegates were noted.

In the aforementioned example, implementation was recommended in respect of a program for removal of barriers to trade and consumption, and for expansion of market opportunities for primary commodity exports, and in respect of a program on international commodity arrangements. This recommendation was directed to all members of the United Nations. Special recommendations were then

addressed to certain groups of countries; they were geared
to the particular economic and trade relationships which
exist between developed market economies and developing countries on the one hand, and between developed centrally planned economy countries and developing countries
on the other hand.

Appendices to the report contained the Report of Working Party 1, a statement by the representative of FAO on
the subject of synthetics and substitutes, suggestions by
some delegates on compensatory financing, and guide lines
on the principles of commodity policy.

The Second Committee

At its Second Plenary Meeting, the Conference designated the Second Committee to deal with trade in manufactures and semi-manufactures. Measures were proposed
to carry out three policies: 1. Diversification and expansion of the export of manufactures and semi-manufactures
by developing countries, with a view to increasing their
share in world trade; 2. Expansion of markets of developing countries; and 3. Promotion of trade in manufactures
and semi-manufactures among developing countries. A-
mong the measures proposed was the establishment of
international machinery for industrial development.

Records of the sixty-two meetings held by the Second
Committee cover the period March 23 to June 4, 1964.[32]

A large number of documents were submitted to the
Committee, consisting of general reference papers, such
as reports by the Preparatory Committee and the group
of experts appointed by the Secretary General of the United Nations; studies of general problems in exports, prepared by international organizations and individual experts;
nine country studies; five different industry studies; and a
document dealing with employment aspects.

The report[33] started with an Introduction in which
the organization of the work was explained. The next section bore the title "Issues before the Committee", and gave
detailed consideration to each of the problems that fell
within the scope of the Committee. The observations made
by the participating delegates, and their attitude toward
certain aspects of questions discussed, were compared
with the statements made by the Secretary General of the
Conference and by other international officials. "As a

rule, the draft recommendations adopted by the Committee in their final form reflect, to the maximum extent possible, the assumption of various views put forward by delegations both in the Committee and in the Plenary Meetings of the Conference. Frequently they are the result of a merging of various proposals."[34]

The draft proposals and counterproposals submitted by individual delegates and by groups of nations were so numerous that it was deemed advisable to set up working groups for the examination of proposals tabled under certain headings and subheadings, "to consolidate, coordinate and amalgamate" proposals wherever possible.[35] In many instances, the Committee decided to have votes by roll call and the delegates submitted statements to explain their vote or their abstention. An "Annex" to the report provides the reader with a synoptic record of such tabled proposals. The report has a table of contents which facilitates a study of its components.

The Third Committee

Within the scope of the Third Committee were a number of topics. One was improvement of the invisible trade of developing countries; another was the matter of financing for an expansion of international trade; and a third was the technical aspect of international compensatory financing and measures for stabilization of primary export earnings at adequate levels.[36]

The report of the Third Committee is very well presented and effectively organized into chapters, sections, subsections, reflecting clearly the Committee's activities.[37]

Six of the Third Committee's sixty-four meetings were devoted to a general debate.[38] This debate helped to reveal where the main interest of the majority of participating delegations was focused, facilitated the task of setting up a program of work and gave the participants the opportunity to become acquainted with each other's point of view.

In an introductory chapter, the report described this procedure. The second chapter gave a summary of the debate. It stressed the fact that the thirty-five participating delegates represented the major geographical areas of the world and each of the principal groups of countries

attending the Conference. The second section of that chapter
listed the draft of proposals submitted to the Committee
by the delegations; it also described the reaction with which
these suggestions were received by other delegates, their
counterproposals and recommendations and the procedure
outlined for promulgation of the proposals.

The detailed points which were raised during the debate on many issues, differentiating the view of one group
or one type of country from another, served in many instances to show even more clearly the basic agreement
on many issues, and at the same time gave an indication
as to what aspects of specific economic problems had been
neglected so far.

For example, a draft recommendation was submitted by the delegations of Argentina, Ceylon, Chile, Colombia, Ecuador, India, Indonesia, Mexico, Nigeria, Syria, the United Arab Republic, the United States of America and Yugoslavia which dealt with the establishment of
a general framework for financial cooperation between developed and developing countries. The report stated that

> The proposal was favorably commented upon by
> many representatives from both developed and
> developing countries as a comprehensive and
> well balanced basis for international financial
> cooperation. It was suggested by some speak-
> ers that once agreement was reached on this
> recommendation, more concrete measures for
> the benefit of the developing countries might
> be adopted. Some speakers observed that al-
> though the ideas presented in the act were es-
> sentially not new, it was desirable to consol-
> idate them and to have them endorsed by the
> Conference. Participation by a major devel-
> oped country as a co-sponsor of the draft was
> welcomed by several speakers from develop-
> ing countries as a sign of political will on the
> part of developed countries to continue and ex-
> pand their efforts. The hope was expressed
> that other developed countries would find it pos-
> sible to give their support to the proposal. [39]

Following this expression of agreement on the basic
proposition, a number of speakers voiced their dissent.

There were requests to treat certain specific items in a
different way; there was a suggestion to make the draft
more concrete; there was apprehension that the time chosen for the proposal was not opportune; there was a demand for clarification of some recommendations. These
and other comments came in part from developed and in
part from developing nations. In addition, representatives
of Communist nations proposed some changes in the text,
mainly designed to shift the emphasis of proposals and to
broaden the approach to specific problems.

These and other representations by a number of countries led to the submission of a revised draft recommendation which took into account several of the suggestions made
during the debate. The delegates voted on the revised draft
recommendation and, when it was approved, the Committee included it in the Annex of its report, for submission
to the Conference.

Essentially, with minor variations according to the
type of problems involved, the procedure outlined above
was followed by the Third Committee throughout its meetings.

The third chapter of the report presented the "Consideration of Proposals", devoting one section to each
issue and subsections to each individual question.

Chapter four contained a summary and conclusions:
a concise two-page statement of the major questions identified, of the areas in which an agreement could be reached.
The Committee attempted to define its own contribution to
the aims of the Conference by describing the type of action
taken during its sessions.

> First, the general targets on which the interna-
> tional community might focus in dealing with the
> problem of development through trade and inter-
> national cooperation in general were appraised.
> Second, a number of principles and criteria,
> aimed at providing constructive guidelines for
> policies in the various areas of international fi-
> nancial and technical cooperation were formu-
> lated; and third, specific measures which could
> bear on the broad issues before the Committee
> were elaborated. [40]

Two Annexes, one constituting draft recommenda-

tions approved by the Committee, the other reporting on
the Working Party on Shipping, concluded the report of
the Third Committee.

The Fourth Committee

The Fourth Committee was set up to explore institutional arrangements, as well as methods and machinery
to implement measures relating to the expansion of international trade. In forty-one meetings between April 17
and June 5, 1964, the two aspects of this problem were
studied, to reappraise the effectiveness of existing international bodies, and the advisability of eliminating overlapping and duplication by coordination and consolidation
of their activities. [41]

In addition to the customary documentation provided
by experts and by international organizations, the Committee also had before it a draft resolution submitted by Czechoslovakia, Poland, and the Union of Soviet Socialist Republics on the creation of an international trade organization, [42]
and a memorandum prepared by the Soviet Union of preliminary considerations regarding the main provisions for
an international trade organization. [43]

The submission of these two documentations was highly significant. It indicated one of the few issues brought
before the Conference on which the opinions of delegates
diverged and on which the Communist bloc presented recommendations basically different. Even at the time when
the U. S. S. R. was ready to join in the activities of international organizations, it did not participate in the General
Agreement on Tariffs and Trade. The U. S. S. R. and the
other nations of the Soviet group did not believe that even
a complete reorganization would enable GATT to function
as an effective instrument on behalf of developing nations.
The creation of a new international trade organization under the auspices of the United Nations was therefore sponsored by the Communist countries.

When the General Debate opened, the delegates to
the Fourth Committee were aware of this basic difference
in opinion. It became clear that "there was general consensus that the existing machinery does not cover all international trade and related problems, particularly those
affecting developing countries . . . that the existing institutions were inadequate and were not equipped with appro-

priate mechanisms to promote such cooperation. "44 It appeared that many delegates were concerned with a variety of aspects of the problem. Some believed that the proliferation of institutions would lead to a dispersion of responsibilities and to overlapping of activities. They also contended that there was lack of coordination and the absence of an integrated and comprehensive framework within which an effective trade and economic development policy could be evolved. Many delegates doubted that any single existing international institution would be able to handle all the relevant problems in the field of trade and development.

There was no general agreement about the underlying causes of such deficiencies, and it remained doubtful whether the replacement of the old machinery regarded as ineffective by new improved institutions would actually alter the basic situation. This development, as some delegates pointed out, was due to the fact that the mere existence of international machinery was not sufficient. An essential ingredient was the political will of the participating governments to carry out the decisions adopted within an international organization. New institutions, it was argued, would be effective only if the member nations were ready and willing to put them into operation.

A statement made by the Executive Secretary of GATT introduced a debate on the activities of that organization and of its potential value. Other international organizations were also discussed, for instance the International Monetary Fund and the International Bank for Reconstruction and Development.

When, at the conclusion of the debate, the delegates took a stand on the question of international arrangements, there was one smaller group which favored the continuance of existing bodies, provided appropriate modifications were made in their terms of reference, practices and activities, so as to enable them to cope with problems of international trade as an instrument of economic development. A larger group of delegates suggested that the existing machinery should be drastically altered, and that the Conference should recommend a new and broader organizational base for international trade. Virtually all delegations of both groups wished to see the establishment of periodic conferences on trade and development, a standing committee and a secretariat, although there was no

agreement as to whether or not this structure should be
of a transitional or permanent character.

The above proceedings were described in the preamble of the report issued by the Fourth Committee.

The next section presented four proposals on institutional arrangements, and a tabulated comparison of these
proposals was included in the Annex of the report. Three
of these proposals called for the creation of an international trade organization, and two of them also envisaged a
transitional arrangement as described above. The fourth
proposal suggested a scheme of periodic conferences, a
standing committee and a permanent secretariat as an
integral part of the United Nations economic machinery
in accordance with Chapters IX and X of the Charter.

In line with the majority decision, reached in the
Fourth Committee, its report to the Conference recommended the establishment of an international trade organization. In view of technical difficulties connected with
the setting up of legal instruments required for the creation of a new organization with broad powers, the report
recommended that, meanwhile, the Conference on Trade
and Development be maintained as a continuing institution,
to be convened periodically, and that a standing committee and a permanent secretariat be established to serve it.

The Fifth Committee

In forty-seven meetings, the Fifth Committee dealt
with the question of expansion of international trade and
its significance for economic development, and with the
implications of regional economic groupings. [45]

The statements made by delegates during the general debate of the Plenary Meetings of the Conference had
drawn attention to the special problems faced by landlocked
countries. The Fifth Committee recognized the importance
of this situation and established a subcommittee of landlocked countries, composed of representatives from forty
governments. The subcommittee held nineteen meetings
from April 6, to May 15, 1964. The report of the subcommittee was submitted to the Fifth Committee, which
considered it in its recommendations to the Conference
and attached it to its report.

Within the terms of reference defined by the Fifth
Committee, the subcommittee studied the problem in four

private meetings which were **accessible** to members of countries which were not members of the subcommittee, and in subsequent public meetings. At the tenth meeting, a working group was established to take into consideration the proposals so far prepared and to draw up for submission a body of principles, designed to promote the transit trade of landlocked states. At its fifteenth meeting, a second working group was set up to study proposals other than those concerning principles. This second working group was also requested to prepare a recommendation on which the subcommittee might act.

As a result of a set of principles submitted by the first task force and of some amendments which delegations had added, the subcommittee formulated eight principles and an interpretative note, explaining that these principles were interrelated, and stressing the cooperative spirit in which they were conceived and in which they must be understood. [46]

The subcommittee also considered the draft prepared by the second working group, and on that basis adopted a recommendation to the Fifth Committee. It suggested the appointment of a committee of twenty-four members representing landlocked, transit and other interested states as governmental experts and on the basis of equitable geographical distribution to prepare a new draft convention to solve the problems of landlocked nations. [47] It further suggested that this draft convention be submitted for consideration and adoption to a conference of plenipotentiaries in 1965.

These recommendations, prepared by the subcommittee, formed part of the Fifth Committee's report to the Conference. [48]

The Committee further established a working group to draft a set of principles governing international trade relations and trade policies conducive to development. This task force, conducting its study through a number of "working parties", developed principles. Proposals were submitted by delegations, studied within the group and accepted, if not unanimously, at least by a considerable number of countries. The report issued by the Working Group, stating the principles agreed on, appeared in an Annex to the Report of the Fifth Committee.

On the basis of the studies conducted by the various task forces and of draft resolutions submitted by a large

number of nations, the Committee made its decisions and
reported them in accordance with the itemized list in the
Preparatory Committee's agenda. The Fifth Committee
Report restated in each instance the essential issue posed,
referred to draft proposals and recommendations which it
had considered, and gave its own conclusions for submission to the Conference.

3. THE FINAL ACT

The Document

At its twenty-fifth Plenary Meeting, on May 6, 1964,
the Conference approved the composition of the Drafting
Committee which, within the recommendations of the General Committee, was responsible for the drafting of the
Final Act. On June 15, 1964, at its thirty-fifth Plenary
Meeting, the Conference adopted the Final Act. [49] This
was the "concise, integrated and consistent" document[50]
that would justify the efforts made to assemble most of
the nations of the world and to utilize their talent, imagination and goodwill in behalf of the improvement of trade
and development.

In a preamble, the Final Act recalled the background
of the Conference. Referring to the United Nations Charter, it declared that "the State signatories of this Final Act
are resolved, in a sense of human solidarity, 'to employ
international machinery for the promotion of the economic
and social advancement of all people'". [51]

The Final Act then sketched existing conditions,
the areas of concern, and the targets set. It restated the
object of the Conference, namely, "to provide by means
of international cooperation appropriate solutions to the
problems of world trade in the interest of all peoples and
particularly to the urgent trade and development problems
of developing countries."[52] At the conclusion of Section I
the determination of the participating states was expressed
to do their utmost to lay the foundation of a better world
economic order.

Section II outlined the constitution of proceedings. It
traced the steps which led to the gathering in Geneva, start-
ing from the first suggestion by the General Assembly in

December, 1961, through the sessions of the Preparatory
Committee, and culminating in the opening meetings in
March, 1964.

Section III set forth the findings by which the Conference was guided. This was a presentation of the problems
which beset the developing countries and their relations
with other nations. It described the efforts made by developed as well as developing countries, by free market
as well as by centrally planned economies, to accelerate
the process of developing and to close the trade gap. It
discussed the inadequacy of measures taken in the past
and the insufficiency of cooperation extended up to now.

This analysis led to Section IV: to an examination of
the factors which caused such problems and contributed
to the difficulties. This section contained the discussion
of these underlying factors and conditions.

The four sections represented the first part of the
Final Act. They were in the nature of an introduction to
the second part, which was the core of the work performed
by the Conference.

Section I of the Second Part gave the principles governing international trade relations and trade policies,
conducive to development. These were principles which
were worked out by the Fifth Committee. Another set of
principles, accompanied by an interpretative note, followed, which also had been proposed by the Fifth Committee, based on the study of special needs for landlocked
countries. Section II dealt with international commodity
problems and enumerated two groups of provisions which
it considered necessary to increase the export earnings of
developing countries: (1) provisions for international commodity arrangements with a basic objective of stimulating
a dynamic and steady growth and insuring reasonable pre-
dictability in the real export earnings of the developing countries, and (2) provision for a program of measures and
actions for the removal of obstacles and discriminatory
practices and for an expansion of market opportunities for
primary commodity exports and for increase in the consumption and imports in developed countries. The Conference recommended that the governments concerned take
practical steps "at the earliest possible date" to implement
these provisions.

Trade in manufactures and semi-manufactures was
the subject of Section III; the recommendations aimed at

the diversification and expansion of the export trade of developing countries as a means of accelerating their economic development and raising their standard of living.

Section IV covered the problem of financing expansion of international trade, and improvement of the invisible trade of developing countries, and included recommendations aimed not only at new and improved measures but also at further study of certain aspects of financing.

Section V recommended institutional arrangements. The most noteworthy provision here was for the establishment of the Conference on Trade and Development as an organ of the General Assembly, to be convened at certain stated intervals. The structure and the functions of this proposed institutional arrangement were outlined.

These first five sections of the Second Part corresponded substantially to the problems which the Preparatory Committee had included in its provisional agenda and which the Plenary Meetings of the Conference had assigned to the five committees. Their recommendations and provisions, presented in the Final Act, were closely following the findings and draft proposals of these committees. Problem areas, studied in committees, which did not fit into any of the above five headings, were combined into Section VI.

In each of the six sections, the Final Act not only pointed out what steps were considered necessary to accomplish the goals set, but in some instances also recommended a specific program which the governments concerned should follow in the future. Further suggestions for such work programs were presented in Section VII.

Three Annexes completed the Final Act: Annex A which reprinted the recommendations of the Conference, as they came out of committees, with the roll call on principles; Annex B, which gave the observations of delegates - some submitted by individual countries, others by groups of nations; Annex C which was made up of messages from heads of states and of a communication, dated June 10, 1964, from the Union of Soviet Socialist Republics, Czechoslovakia and Poland, on the possible future development of trade between the socialist countries and the developing countries.

On June 16, 1964, delegates of one hundred and eighteen governments[53] signed the Final Act which was then deposited with the Secretary General of the United Nations.

The Closing of the Conference

The thirty-fifth Plenary Meeting which adopted the Final Act, also instructed the Rapporteur to prepare a Report of the United Nations Conference on Trade and Development.[54] That Report consisted of a factual account, giving the background and constitution of the Conference, the reports of the five committees, as adopted by the committees and noted by the Conference, a report of action taken by the Plenary Meetings on the recommendations of the committees and of relevant texts.

In accordance with a decision made at the twenty-fifth Plenary Meeting of the Conference, the Final Act and the Report were later issued as a single document.[55]

The close of the Conference was marked by a joint declaration, issued by seventy-seven developing nations. It was a statement which expressed the mixed feelings the Conference had evoked among the members of that group: appreciation for the endeavor of developed governments to cooperate in behalf of trade and development; disappointment that some of the major problems raised had not been adequately resolved; and hope that the results of the Conference would lay the foundation for more substantial progress in the period ahead. Striking an optimistic note, the declaration stated that the United Nations Conference on Trade and Development marked the beginning of a new era in the evolution of international cooperation of trade and development.

After statements by the Secretary General of the Conference and by its President, the fifty-sixth Plenary Meeting of June 16, 1964, came to an end and the President declared the United Nations Conference on Trade and Development closed.[56]

The Final Act and Report, issued by the Conference, were submitted to the thirty-seventh session of the Economic and Social Council which reviewed them. The Council resolved unanimously to take into consideration the recommendations of the Conference in so far as they related to its work, and invited the specialized agencies to take into account the recommendations of the Conference in preparing their work programs.[57]

ECOSOC transmitted the Final Act and Report to the General Assembly at its nineteenth session for further action.

CHAPTER **6** INSTITUTIONALIZATION
OF THE CONFERENCE

1. NEW SPECIALIZED AGENCY

The description of the working methods pursued by
the Second Committee[1] touched on the fact that there was
basic agreement on many issues, while at the same time
the participating delegations differed about details and
about methods of implementation.

This divergence was illustrated by the positions which
the delegates took on the important question of international machinery for industrial development. The report of
the Second Committee stated that

> developing countries are . . . in need of ad-
> visory, technical and other assistance ren-
> dered both bilaterally by individual developed
> countries and also through appropriate inter-
> national organizations. While there was gen-
> eral agreement on the actions which had to
> be taken on an international level, two views
> on the nature of the international machinery
> . . . emerged in the course of discussions;
> (i) one favoring the establishment of a United
> Nations specialized agency for this purpose;
> and (ii) the other recommending an enlarge-
> ment of the functions and strengthening of the
> resources of the existing Center for Interna-
> tional Development within the framework of
> the Department of Economic and Social Af-
> fairs of the United Nations.[2]

Actually, the two proposals which were put to the
vote by the Second Committee represented a compromise
reached after some other suggestions had been withdrawn.

The roll call on this item revealed another striking
phenomenon which brought to mind the "united front" of
developing countries to which the delegate from Brazil
had referred.[3] The draft recommendation adopted by the

Second Committee for submission to the Conference called
for a new specialized agency. The plan was sponsored
by thirty-seven developing nations. The fifty-eight nations which voted in favor of the proposal were - with the
exception of the Soviet bloc - more or less underdeveloped
countries. The votes against the creation of a new specialized agency were cast by twenty-one countries of which
twenty were developed. There were six abstentions of
varied origin. When the Conference adopted the recommendation with eighty-one for to twenty-three against and
eight abstentions, the distribution was similar. [4]
    Belgium, one of the countries which cast a vote a-
gainst the new agency, justified its position by stating that
it favored a dynamic program for industrial development,
and therefore wished to see the Center for Industrial Development to become a catalyst for the industrial development of the developing countries. [5] Luxemburg agreed
with this observation. [6]
    The recommendation adopted by the Conference
called upon the General Assembly to take suitable action
for the establishment of a specialized agency for industrial development, to assume functions such as the com-
pilation, interpretation and publication of information concerning industrial technology, production, programming
and planning, cooperation with existing regional economic
commissions, promotion of national, regional and international action to speed up industrial development of developing countries, study of the formulation of credit policies to promote the industrial expansion of developing countries and to stimulate their exports of manufactures and
semi-manufactures, research, technical assistance and
cooperation with other specialized agencies.
    Pending the establishment of the new agency, the
Center was assigned to fulfill these functions.

2.   PERMANENT BODY AS ORGAN OF U. N.

    In the statement that Dr. Raul Prebisch had made at
the twenty-fifth Plenary Meeting, on May 6, 1964, he referred to the magnitude of the task which the Conference
had undertaken. He expressed his gratification over the
quality and quantity of recommendations submitted by the

participating nations. However, he also showed concern
over the very limited time left until the closing day of the
Conference, June 14, 1964, since it seemed to him doubtful that within the remaining few weeks all the issues raised
in these recommendations could be explored. Dr. Prebisch therefore suggested that only such proposals be considered by the Conference as had a direct bearing on the
central issue. He defined the central issue as the fact
that any national attempt to accelerate the rate of growth
of underdeveloped economies met with tremendous obstacles "from outside". Terming this phenomenon the "basic problem of the so-called trade gap", he proposed that
it serve as the criterion in deciding on the priority to be
accorded to the recommendations submitted during the
last weeks of the Conference. [7]

The convocation of the Conference, the General Debate and the work of the Committees, and the attention
which these activities had received throughout the world,
had stimulated many governments to consider possibilities for solving economic problems of developing countries and to make constructive recommendations. The
Conference machinery was unable to cope with that material to the extent that it had no direct bearing on the Conference itself, even though it was closely connected with
its ultimate aims; some international body should be found
to follow up on the suggestions made in the wide area of
financial and technical cooperation, with the increasing
burden of accumulated debt and service payments and other related problems.

Aside from these practical considerations, and on
the basis of its own study, the Fourth Committee came
to the conclusion that the establishment of permanent machinery was necessary.

It has been mentioned previously that one of the most
controversial issues at the Conference was the extent to
which GATT served or could serve a useful purpose. Obviously, the General Agreement on Tariffs and Trade had
not solved all problems in the area of trade and development, since it was thought necessary to call a special conference on trade and development. The question which
arose in the course of debates was therefore not whether
GATT in its present form should be retained, or could be
expected to solve such problems. The issue on which the
participating nations were divided was whether there was

any promise in reforming GATT or whether that organization was conceptually not fit to promote trade and development in behalf of developing countries. [8]

The General Agreement on Tariffs and Trade

As of 1964, seventy-four nations had established
some relationship with GATT.   There are sixty-two contracting parties, member governments acting jointly, dealing with questions arising from the implementation of the
Agreement and taking such action as is necessary in the
light of developments in international trade to further the
objectives stated in the Agreement; there are five which
have acceeded provisionally; two which have participated
in the work of the contracting parties under special arrangement; and five to whose territories the Agreement has
been applied and which now, as independent states, maintain a de facto application of the GATT pending final decisions as to their future commercial policy.
The roster of these participants included countries
in all parts of the world and at all stages of development.
This list also indicated that membership was not confined
to countries with free market economies but extended to
centrally planned economies, although the principal Communist power, the U.S.S.R., remained outside the GATT.
The twenty-three nations of the Atlantic Community
and Latin America which met in Geneva in 1947, entered
into a multilateral treaty which became known as GATT,
embodying reciprocal rights and obligations, designed to
achieve certain objectives.   The preamble of the General
Agreement described the aims of the contracting parties
as follows: to conduct their relations in the field of trade
and economic endeavor "with a view to raising standards
of living, insuring full employment and a large steadily
growing volume of real income and effective demand, developing the full use of the resources of the world and ex-
panding the production and exchange of goods and promot-
ing the progressive development of the economies of all
the contracting parties. "
The primary purpose of the General Agreement was
not geared to relieve the special problems of developing
countries, but was guided by general trade principles, such
as the "most favored nation" principle; the policy to afford
protection to domestic industries exclusively through cus-

toms tariffs with the tendency to reduce such tariffs gradually; the use of consultation in case of disputes and the
institution of joint action to further the objectives of the
agreement. Some of these principles could be expected
to yield favorable results for developed and developing
countries alike; some of these, however, would put the
developing nations under obligations that might run contrary to the interests of their economies.

    This fact led to a number of amendments and addi-
tions to the General Agreement, aimed at taking into account the needs of developing countries. In that spirit,
changes in the General Agreement were made in 1954-
1955. Subsequently, Trade Ministers' Meetings during
the years 1957 and 1958 were increasingly interested in
trade and economic development of developing countries ;
and the Program for Trade Expansion, initiated in 1958,
gave these problems an important place on its agenda. One
of three committees organized for the implementation of
the Program was to study expansion possibilities in the
export earnings of less developed countries. Another step
in the same direction was the adoption of a declaration by
the contracting parties on December 7, 1961, to promote
the trade of the less developed countries. Moreover, a
resolution was adopted at a Meeting of Ministers on May 21,
1963, for the introduction of measures toward the expansion of the trade of developing countries as a means of
furthering their economic development.

    The "Kennedy Round", as these negotiations have
been called, were intended to be different from previous
meetings, and to be more ambitious in their objectives.
They were designed to reduce and ultimately to remove
the existing trade barriers in order to help in reaping the
benefits of modern technology and to promote trade relations with regional groupings. This was of immediate concern to developed countries only. The plan envisaged, however, as a further step in the program the extension of
the most-favored-nation principle to developing countries
without the requirement of full reciprocity. Another important innovation was the inclusion of all categories of
goods, including agricultural products in the trade negotiations. [9]

    All these attempts did not succeed in altering the ba-
sic character of the General Agreement sufficiently - at
least not in the opinion of all the delegates to the Confer-

ence on Trade and Development. They were united in their
opinion that GATT "had not fully realized the trade policy
and economic growth requirement of the less developed
countries". [10] Many delegations blamed the failure of
GATT's reform movement on the reluctance of some contracting parties to agree on important issues. Although
some delegates were optimistic about the outlook, and still
believed that future changes in the structure and policy of
the General Agreement might benefit the trade and development of developing countries, the majority were inclined
to look for other solutions.

The New Institutional Arrangement

At its twenty-eighth Plenary Meeting, the Conference took note of the report submitted by the Fourth Committee, [11] and at its thirty-fifth Plenary Meeting, it dealt
with the draft recommendation of the Fourth Committee
as well as with another draft recommendation, submitted
by the President of the Conference. [12] As a result, a draft
recommendation was worked out "on the institutional arrangements, method and machinery to implement measures relating to the expansion of international trade"[13]
which suggested that the Conference on Trade and Development be established as an organ of the United Nations General Assembly; that a Trade and Development Board be
set up as a permanent organ of the Conference; and that
arrangements be made to organize a Secretariat which
would service the Conference, the Board and its subsidiary bodies.

Members of the United Nations, of the specialized
agencies and of the Atomic Energy Commission would constitute the membership of the Conference.

To this first provision of the constitutional arrangement, the delegation of Burma took exception. It pointed
out that the criteria laid down for membership in the permanent Conference did not conform to the principles of
universality which the Preparatory Committee had taken
for its guide; and claimed that not even an attempt was
made to come as near to universality as possible. [14] In
a joint declaration submitted by Bulgaria, Czechoslovakia,
Hungary, Poland and the U.S.S.R., these nations expressed
the view that the membership provision did not reflect the
substance of proposals and statements made during the Con-

ference meetings. [15]

The second paragraph of the draft recommendation provided that the new body should meet at intervals of not more than three years at a date and location determined by the General Assembly.

The draft recommendation of the Conference also embodied seven principal functions as follows:

(a) to promote international trade, especially with a view to accelerating economic development, particularly trade between countries at different stages of development, between developing countries and between countries with different systems of economic and social organization, taking into account the functions performed by existing international organizations;

(b) to formulate principles and policies on international trade and related problems of economic development;

(c) to make proposals for putting the said principles and policies into effect and to take such other steps within its competence as may be relevant to this end, having regard to differences in economic systems and stages of development;

(d) generally, to review and facilitate the coordination of activities of other institutions within the United Nations system in the field of international trade and related problems of economic development and in this regard to cooperate with the General Assembly and the Economic and Social Council in respect to the performance of their Charter responsibilities for coordination;

(e) to initiate action, where appropriate, in cooperation with the competent organs of the United Nations for the negotiation and adoption of multilateral legal instruments in the field of trade, with due regard to the adequacy of existing organs of negotiation and without duplication of their activities;

(f) to be available as a center for harmonizing the trade and related documents on development policies of governments and regional economic

groupings in pursuance of Art. 1 of the United Nations Charter; and
(g) to deal with any other matter within the scope
of its competence.[16]

In this list of functions, the Conference showed its
awareness of the dangers inherent in the creation of a new
institution in the field of economic development. Since the
existence of duplication and overlapping had long been a
concern of international administrators, an additional organization within the United Nations system might easily
bring more problems than relief, unless special precau-
tionary measures were taken. These measures were explicitly suggested in sections (a), (d), and (e) of the above
summary.
Paragraphs four to twenty-four of the draft recommendation dealt with the composition and the functions of
the Trade and Development Board. Of special interest
was the attempt to base the selection of board members
on principles which were considered fair in two respects:
with regard to equitable geographical distribution, and
with regard to continuing representation for the principal
trading states. In order to achieve this aim, a certain
number of members were to be taken from four different
groups of nations, listed in the recommendation: twenty-
two from sixty-one developing countries in Asia, Africa,
the Middle East and the Far East; eighteen from twenty-
nine developed states; nine from twenty-two Latin American nations; and six from nine countries with centrally
planned economies in Eastern and Central Europe.[17]
Burma raised an objection to this distribution, con-
tending that less than adequate representation was given
to the developing countries.[18]
The draft recommendation gave the rules governing
the election for the representation of intergovernmental
bodies and subsidiary agencies who would participate -
without vote - in its deliberations. The Board was em-
powered to make its own rules of procedure and to determine the frequency of its meetings, although it was expected to meet normally twice in any one year. The functions of the Board included the implementation of recommendations and other decisions made by the Conference;
the initiation of studies and reports in the field of trade
and related problems; the coordination with other inter-

national and intergovernmental organizations and their activities and reports; the preparation of future sessions of
the Conference; and an Annual Report to the General Assembly through the Economic and Social Council.

Paragraph twenty-three provided for the establishment of subsidiary organs that would assist the Board in
the discharge of its functions, and it named in particular
three areas that would require such action: the regulation
of commodities, of manufactures, and financing related
to trade. In that connection, the recommendation again
referred to the necessity of coordinating the activities of
the new organ with those of the established international
agencies.

The procedure for voting was regulated in paragraph
twenty-four. It was based on the principle of "one country: one vote", and required a two-thirds majority of those
present and voting in decisions of the Conference on matters of substance. Decisions of the Conference in procedural matters, and all decisions of the Board, required
only a simple majority of those present and voting.

Of all the provisions contained in the draft recommendation on institutional arrangements, the twenty-fifth paragraph aroused the most comment. It dealt with the process
of conciliation proposed within the United Nations Conference on Trade and Development. The details of the recommendation, and the comments it aroused, will be discussed
in the next Section of this Chapter.

The draft recommendation, moreover, called for ar-
rangements to prepare the immediate establishment of an
"adequate permanent and full time Secretariat within the
United Nations Secretariat" to be headed by the Secretary
General of the Conference. The Secretary General of the
United Nations would appoint the Secretary General of the
Conference, with the approval of the General Assembly. [19]

A separate budgetary provision was to be made within the regular United Nations budget to cover the expenses
of the Conference, its subsidiary bodies and its Secretariat. In two paragraphs, future institutional arrangements
were mentioned. The Conference was to review the "effectiveness and further evolution of the institutional arrangements with a view to recommending such changes and
improvements as might be necessary"; and to this end should
study "matters relating to the establishment of a comprehensive organization . . . to deal with trade and with trade

in relation with development".

In the joint statement of the Soviet bloc, mentioned above, [20] attention was drawn to the fact that "the majority of those participating in the Conference clearly favored the speedy establishment of a universal international trade organization . . . ." In the introduction to the draft recommendation, submitted to the General Assembly, the Conference itself took note "of the widespread desire among developing countries for a comprehensive trade organization", and it can be assumed that this fact prompted the Conference to instruct the permanent organization to study the possibilities of establishing an agency which would deal with trade. The reservation raised by Bulgaria, Czechoslovakia, Hungary, Poland and the U.S.S.R. indicated that the response to this request was not considered sufficiently prompt.

Another observation submitted to the same provision, that of Burma, stressed the point that the membership of a comprehensive trade organization, as envisaged for the future, should not follow the membership rules of the permanent Conference, but should be open to all states of the world in order to ensure international cooperation. [21]

Another delegation which went on record with a special remark on the proposed institutional arrangement was that of Britain, which warned that the interests of the developing countries could be effectively served only if the agreements of individual countries concerned would be sought, whether these were developed or developing; and that regard for national sovereignty and legitimate economic interest should be observed. [22]

In spite of the reservations expressed by the above countries, the Conference participants endorsed the draft recommendation. The institutional arrangements, as proposed by the Fourth Committee, were adopted by the Conference without dissent.

No such unanimity was achieved with respect to two other recommendations based on proposals of the Fourth Committee. One dealt with institutional arrangements during the interim period, between the conclusion of the Conference and the recommended action of the General Assembly. It requested the Secretary General of the United Nations to take appropriate measures, including the necessary financial steps, in order to start without delay the work required for the implementation of the Confer-

ence recommendations. The recommendation was adopted
by seventy-seven votes, while fifteen votes were cast a-
gainst it and nine countries abstained from voting.

The second recommendation which received a mixed
reception was concerned with the terms of reference of
subsidiary organs to be established by the Trade and Development Board of the Conference. Voting revealed se-
venty-nine for, fourteen against the recommendation, with
ten abstentions.

Action by the General Assembly

The recommendations on institutional arrangements
adopted by the Conference formed the basis for a draft resolution submitted to the General Assembly of the United
Nations by its President. On December 30, 1964, this resolution was adopted without objection.

3.   CONCILIATION MACHINERY

The Recommendation

The recommendation for institutional arrangements
formulated by the Conference and contained in its Final
Act, Annex A, V, 1, provided under the heading "Procedures", in paragraph 25:

It is recommended that the provisions of this paragraph shall be determined by the General Assembly at its nineteenth session after consideration
by it of the report and proposals to be made by a
Special Committee to be appointed by the Secretary General of the United Nations, as indicated
in item (d) of the Transitional Provisions.
The terms of reference of this Special Committee would be as follows:
(a) The task of the Committee shall be to prepare
    proposals for procedures within the continuing
    machinery designed to establish a process of
    conciliation to take place before voting and to
    provide an adequate basis for the adoption of
    recommendations with regard to proposals of

a specific nature for actions substantially affecting the economic and financial interests of
particular countries;
(b) such conciliation may be carried out through
a system of conciliation committees, the good
offices of the Secretary General of the Conference, or any other means within the framework
of the United Nations;
(c) in devising the procedures referred to above,
the Committee shall take into consideration
that the interested states may wish to state and
publicize their views. It shall also take into
account the desirability of issuing reports at
appropriate times which would state the areas
of agreement and disagreement and the explan-
ation of positions as regards, in particular,
the implementation of proposed recommendations;
(d) the Committee should also consider the desirability of applying appropriate procedures to
proposals involving changes in the fundamental provisions of this resolution; and
(e) any government participating in this Conference may submit to the Special Committee such
proposals and recommendations as it considers
relevant to subsection (a) above, provided they
do not imply any amendment to the Charter of
the United Nations or any departure from the
principle that each country has one vote. The
Special Committee shall include a study of such
proposals and recommendations in its report
to the General Assembly.

The above recommendation was based on the conclusion, arrived at by the Conference participants, that special conciliation procedures might be useful to promote
wider agreement on important issues which might come before future sessions of the Conference.

It should be noted that the recommendation not only
expressed the main concern of the majority to establish
conciliation before voting on certain important issues. The
formulation of guidelines to the Special Committee also
clearly enunciated the desire of the majority of nations to
safeguard the principle "one country: one vote", as shown

in the provision that proposals submitted should "not imply
any departure from the principle that each country has one
vote". [23]

Under the provisions outlined in sections (a) to (e)
of paragraph 25, the Secretary General of the United Nations, in autumn, 1964, appointed a Special Committee of
twelve members. The selection was made "on an equitable geographical basis, after consultation with the respective governments". [24] These members served in their personal capacities and were partly diplomats, partly high
officials in governmental departments, and partly experts
in the field of economics.

In his foreword to the Special Committee's Report,
Secretary General U Thant pointed out that "the task set
for the Special Committee was a difficult and complex one.
The members of the Committee have undertaken it with
thoroughness and earnestness and in conciliatory spirit
which is amply reflected in their report. They have come
forward with a unanimous set of recommendations which
I commend to the General Assembly for consideration." [25]

The Special Committee

The Special Committee met at United Nations Head-
quarters during the period September 28 to October 23,
1964. The Secretary General of the Conference, Dr. Raul
Prebisch, was present at the meetings.

When paragraph 25 was adopted by the Conference,
a number of nations made statements: the Federal Republic of Germany, which is not a United Nations member,
voiced the hope that it would be given the opportunity to
express its views on the proposals of the Special Committee before they were submitted to the General Assembly
of the United Nations; [26] Switzerland included in its statement a similar remark; [27] the French delegation found the
provision unnecessarily complicated and advocated "a similar wording which would not have prejudged in any way
the direction in which solutions of difficulties in question
should be solved, or the manner in which a problem should
be settled before any steps have even been taken to study
it." [28] The United States was in favor of the guidelines
submitted to the Special Committee "on the assumption
that such machinery and the procedures to be developed
. . . will be acceptable to the developed as well as to

developing countries."29
    The above statements were as stated, observations
only. They indicated that the countries submitting statements did not object to the provision, but showed their interest in a procedure of conciliation.
    This point was borne out by the fact that additional
texts were submitted by fifteen governments while the matter was under consideration before the Special Committee. Some of these statements merely stressed the importance of conciliation machinery; other statements expressed the point of view held by some nations on general
principles; and some gave detailed proposals on individual
points.30 The report of the Special Committee, submitted to the United Nations General Assembly, reviewed these
proposals, recommendations and observations and summar-
ized them in topical arrangement under headings such as
"voting rights", "voting as a means of ascertaining areas
of agreement", "time limits", "membership and site of
conciliation committees", and others.31
    The Special Committee evaluated the objectives of
conciliation and its character. It classified the proposals
into one group of problems which would call for special conciliation, and another group which would not lend itself
to such action. It formulated both the procedures for special conciliation and the required mechanism. On the basis of its study, the Special Committee submitted a draft
of its proposals to the nineteenth session of the United
Nations General Assembly.

                The Draft Proposal

    The proposal of the Special Committee, submitted
to the General Assembly, was intended to replace paragraph 25 of the recommendation which the Conference had
included in its Final Act. The draft proposal provided for
a process of conciliation for the solution of problems that
substantially affected the economic or financial interests
of particular countries in specific cases. The type of problems which would be subjected to conciliation were enumerated. In addition, one special category of proposals would
require conciliation: namely, proposals involving changes
in the fundamental provisions of the conciliation recommendation itself.
    The process of conciliation could start on the level

of the Conference, of the Board or of its committees, and
the proposal for conciliation could be made upon the request of a certain number of members; it could also be initiated by the President of the Conference and the Chairman
of the Board or of a Committee.

A prerequisite for the use of conciliation was a debate on the proposal; voting was then suspended. Dr. Raul
Prebisch considers the inclusion of the provision that conciliation machinery is to secure agreement between the
parties before a vote is taken as one of the most important accomplishments of UNCTAD.

The President or the Chairman would "as soon as
possible" after consultation with the members of the organ
concerned nominate the members of a conciliation committee and submit the nomination for approval of the Conference or the Board, as appropriate. Conciliation committees were supposed to be small and selected on an equitable geographical basis; they should include countries interested in the subject at issue. Detailed instructions
followed about the procedure within conciliation committees, their reports, and the action required of the Board
and the Conference after conciliation. There was also a
provision that the good offices of the Secretary General
of the Conference should be utilized as fully as practicable
in connection with the process of conciliation.

The President of the General Assembly submitted
to the Assembly at its nineteenth session a draft resolution on the "Establishment of the United Nations Conference on Trade and Development as an Organ of the General Assembly". [32] This document contained the draft
recommendation prepared by the Conference; paragraph
25, however, was replaced by the draft proposal prepared
by the Special Committee. The conciliation machinery,
as devised by the Special Committee, was therefore part
of the institutional arrangements adopted by the United
Nations General Assembly on December 30, 1964.

Pertinent Questions

The evaluation of the results achieved by the United Nations Conference on Trade and Development as an instrument of U.N. diplomacy need not concern itself with the economic measures suggested and the recommendations made in the field of trade and development. A summary of these findings is available in the Report of the Conference[1] and in its Final Act;[2] a Review of Action Taken by the Conference has been published, together with an Appraisal of the Impact which the Conference had on Public Opinion.[3]

For the purpose of this study, other questions seem pertinent. They are concerned, in part, with issues which were not explicitly discussed at any time during the debate or in the committee meetings, yet formed the underlying assumptions of the Conference; in part, they are aimed to aid in the analysis of the concept which seemed to be motivating some delegations; and in part, they are designed to explain a course of action taken by certain nations. The answers to such questions promised to elucidate the meaning of the Conference in terms of U.N. diplomacy. Yet, mere speculation along these lines would be of no real value unless verified by some practical device. The use of a questionnaire seemed to offer means for such verification, to a limited extent at least.

Questionnaires, requesting a personal evaluation by U.N. diplomats on specific issues[4] were in fact distributed to a number of delegates who had in one capacity or another participated in the sessions or the work of the Conference. Care was taken to approach members from East, West and South; representatives of developed as well as developing countries; of free enterprise and centrally planned economies; of the various blocs formed in Africa, the Middle East, Latin America and Asia. Most of these individuals who were requested to answer the questionnaire showed willingness to cooperate. The representatives of eighteen nations[5] provided written answers in great detail. The information thus received proved helpful in adding an informed and, in many cases, an original note to the evaluation of the Conference and its results.

The Accomplishment

The Conference closed on a note of harmony and optimism. The Final Act stated the determination of the participating governments, "taking note of the recommendations
of the Conference, to do their utmost to lay the foundations
of a better world economic order". This resolution expressed an accomplishment as well as a limitation.

The most outstanding achievement of the Conference
lies in the very fact that it could be held; that it could proceed and be concluded without any disruption and that political issues and ideological differences among the participating nations and governments did not disturb the international cooperation and conciliation. This was a situation which, at the outset, did not appear likely and had not
been taken for granted. [6]

When, in the Final Act, the participating governments
expressed their determination to proceed, in the future,
in line with the Conference recommendations, this could be
taken as a promise to keep up the spirit of international
cooperation which had been strengthened, if not actually
created, in Geneva.

The limitation implied in the above resolution is an
inherent feature of conferences in general. For tangible
results, for concrete stipulations, bilateral or multilateral agreements are the proper instruments. What a conference can do is to prepare the atmosphere in which bilateral agreements can be successfully negotiated.

Delegates from developing countries, attending the
Conferences, showed awareness of this limitation by re-
marking that international conferences are effective in
diagnosing the general trends and patterns of economic relationships, and that they can establish an over-all code of
principles guiding international trade in all its aspects.
As one representative from a centrally planned economy
pointed out, international conferences can be useful in pro-
viding a stimulus for the improvement of bilateral relations. A number of diplomats from a variety of countries
agreed that conferences and bilateral agreements comple-
mented each other, and that one could not replace the other. An immediate and direct effect of conference recommendations on trade and development was therefore not

anticipated, and a resolution of participating governments
to take note of the Conference recommendations, such as
the above statement included in the Final Act, was as much
as could be expected.

Yet, in view of the great hopes which the prospect
of the Conference had aroused in the developing countries,
this did not seem enough of an accomplishment.

Permanent Machinery

If it was left to the individual governments to implement the recommendations of the Conference and to solve
the multitude of economic problems which had been analyzed
and studied in the five committees, the brave attempt in
Geneva would indeed have to be considered as merely one
more international conference. The solution was found in
the establishment of permanent machinery.

There is a striking similarity in the analysis of Conference accomplishment, as it was made by a representative of a major power and by a delegate from a developing
country; both recognized two main purposes: 1. the Conference brought about a much clearer understanding of the
needs of developing countries and of their complex economic development problems; 2. the Conference was able
to achieve a compromise solution unanimously approved
for the establishment of new institutions within the United
Nations to continue its work in the future and to deal more
realistically with problems of trade and development.

The establishment of permanent machinery as such
confirmed the continuing faith of the participating nations
in the ultimate effectiveness of the conference technique
within the United Nations system. It was believed that
whatever promise the first meetings had held could be
brought to fulfillment in future sessions.

This development could seem a satisfactory answer
to the expectation and demand expressed at the beginning
of the Conference, on March 23, 1964, by its President,
"that this meeting is not - and cannot be - just another ordinary conference." The Geneva gathering led to the creation of new international organization designed to pursue
new goals within the United Nations system.

Actually, the quest for something new and extraordinary in the field of trade and development can be answered
by the Conference only if the machinery created proved to

be more than merely another international organization.
A survey among diplomats, civil servants and experts
who, having actively participated in the Conference, hold
definite opinions on the subject, seems to indicate that,
at this time, the prevailing approach is marked by cau-
tion. The written answers expressed an attitude that can
best be described as cautiously optimistic. The degree of
optimism varies and so do the reasons advanced for it.

There was apprehension in some quarters that the
new machinery may duplicate the work of the Second Committee of the General Assembly, particularly if its debates
are not attended by qualified delegates; and that this might
increase the political pressure without helping to lead to
practical solutions. Also, that there might be duplication
with specialized international organizations, members of
the U.N. family, founded to perform specific tasks. At
the same time, confidence was expressed that the governments would be conscious of the necessity of establishing
harmonious complementary relations among these various
U.N. bodies so as to ensure that - while UNCTAD really
contributed something new - the resources of all were
used to common advantage.

A slightly different approach to the question of duplication was suggested by the delegate from a Middle Eastern country, who drew attention to the fact that the new institution represents a departure from the concept of a debating forum which is at present provided by the Economic
and Social Council and the Second Committee of the General
Assembly, and that it should provide not only a debating
forum but also a negotiating forum.

These more technical considerations seemed over-
shadowed by a more basic concern, expressed by one of
the representatives of a developing country and echoed
in most replies from emergent nations: that much will
depend on the measure of cooperation which the major
trading powers will extend to the new organ;that the permanent machinery will, like other international organizations, be only as effective as its members make it. And
an expert from a centrally planned economy remarked so-
berly that the machinery can only be as efficient as there
is political will to make it so; and that - judging from the
present political will - one cannot be over-optimistic.

In the discussion of the committee work which led
to the Conference resolution on the establishment of per-

manent machinery, reference was made to observations
and statements by a number of representatives. Two principal aims were sought by some delegations at the time,
although the realization of these aims was not pressed in
the interest of harmony and for the sake of attaining unanimity. One of these was the desire to base membership in the new international organization on the principle of universality; the other was the desire for an international trade organization. Both objectives were still
very much in the minds of some diplomats when discussing
future permanent machinery, and this view found its way
into the replies to the questionnaires. Thus, a delegate
from a Communist country claimed that dynamic development of the new international organization would large-
ly depend on the question whether or not it would become
a comprehensive body with wide competence and universal membership. And a diplomat representing a major
power following the same ideology stated emphatically
that the permanent machinery established by the Conference would add something new and different to U.N. activities and was considered a first step towards the universal international trade organization, open to all states
interested in its work.

The optimistic approach, noticeable in all answers
received as well as in personal interviews with diplomats
from various countries, augurs well for the permanent
organization. It is likely to create a congenial atmosphere
for future meetings, and to make national representatives
receptive to further suggestions.

If, from this point of view, the Conference can be
considered a success, who deserves credit for it?

The Role of International Civil Servants

An international gathering, such as the Conference
on Trade and Development, is not created by the imagination and determination of a single individual. It was,
as Secretary General U Thant explained on March 23, 1964,
"a long chain of events that contributed over many years to
a growing conviction that the United Nations must make a
determined effort to deal jointly with the problems of trade
and development or run the risk of frustrating the efforts
of the organization to maintain world peace. "[7]

Prerequisites for the establishment of the Confer-

ence were a series of earlier conferences, creating the
conference technique; the experience of many countries
in negotiations relating to trade and development to engage
their governments' interest; the realization on the part
of developing countries that their own efforts would remain unsuccessful unless the industrialized nations participated in their planning for future action; the conviction on the part of the developed countries that aid and trade
measures taken in behalf of developing nations would not
prove meaningful unless the developing countries had a
voice in the economic decisions made. This was the setting within which international cooperation and division of
labor could begin.

If one person was more closely connected than any
other with the search for solutions and with the planning
of strategy to tackle them, it was Dr. Raul Prebisch, Secretary General of the Conference on Trade and Development. With his academic background and his experience
as a civil servant of his national Argentina, as well as international civil service, he was adequately equipped for
his post. He steeled himself for the special demands which
preparations for the Conference would make on him by
touring the world to become familiar with trade and development problems outside Latin America, and he became an expert on the special economic problems of developing countries. He has been called the "leading spirit" of the Conference and the program developed by him
in his report "Towards a New Trade Policy for Development", as well as his statements, articles and speeches
cover the wide range of problems with which the Conference dealt. The work of the Preparatory Committee which
he directed was based on his concepts.

The decisive influence which Dr. Prebisch was able
to exercise over the Conference brought to mind the contro-
versy about the role which international civil servants are
supposed to play. The question is often asked whether they
should be confined to **administrative and technical matters.**
The main tasks which occupy **personnel** of the secretariats
of international organizations are undoubtedly connected with
such housekeeping needs, and the question of policy decisions and political interference hardly arises on the lower
levels. For the top-ranking international civil servant,
however, the issue is problematic.

The representative of a Latin American country ex-

pressed the opinion that an examination of political aspects
of international relations should not be entrusted to international civil servants. Another diplomat suggested that
the extent to which the international civil servant's activities extend beyond technical and administrative matters is
determined by the constitution or statutes of the organization to which he belongs.

That this does not necessarily follow has been demonstrated by the experience with a succession of Secretaries General of the United Nations. Under the same
Charter, Trygve Lie delegated most of his administrative
responsibilities, to concentrate on matters of policy; Dag
Hammerskjold took the opposite stand at the beginning of
his term, and altered his approach later, until he finally
emerged as a leading political and diplomatic force; while
the present Secretary General, U Thant, seems to inter-
pret his position in strict conservative terms.

This record suggests that the Secretary General's
approach to the responsibilities of his office is not due
so much to constitutional provisions, and not even to the
course of world events; rather it is the incumbent's view
of his responsibility, and his personal philosophy which
determine his position with the U.N. system.

Measured by the limited sample of diplomatic opinion gathered in interviews and questionnaires, the value
of a capable international civil servant's experience is ap-
preciated and his cooperation is usually welcomed. This
conclusion is borne out by the fact that the Charter of the
new permanent machinery assigns an important place to
its Secretary General: "The good offices of the Secretary
General of the Conference shall be utilized as fully as practicable in connection with the process of conciliation."[8]

The Role of Experts

Another group of persons, closely connected with the
Conference and in great extent responsible for such success
as it achieved, was the economic experts who participated
in its work. It was the tradition of the League and has
also been the tradition of the United Nations to consult experts in their professional and technical capacity, and not
as representatives of the countries of which they were na-
tionals.

As already pointed out, a report prepared by a group

of twelve experts had been submitted to the Preparatory
Committee of the Conference, [9] and a large number of monographs, reports, articles and surveys, prepared by know-
ledgeable persons in fields related to trade and development
had been included in the documentation for work in the five
committees.

Another category of experts participated in the Conference in a more direct way. The delegations sent to the
Conference by member governments included, in many
instances, representatives selected on the basis of their
knowledge in the field of economics. Ministers of Planning,
of Economic Affairs, of Finance, of Agriculture, of Foreign Trade Relations, and of similar government departments attended the Conference as spokesmen for their national policy, and their expertise enabled them to add a
note of authority to their official statements.

Helpful as an educated opinion on the subject under
discussion can be to the government representative participating in the Conference, it will still be up to the professional and technical expert to provide the raw material
for discussion and decision-making. In committees, sub-
committees and in working groups and task forces his
work is indispensable. The representative of one country -
himself an expert - defined the particular quality of the
experts which makes them so valuable in the preparation
of international conferences as the fact that they are able
to take a more general view, that they talk the same language and that they are able to see the common interest
behind the ideological and other political differences.

The task of the expert ends with the advice given to
members of his delegation since - as one Latin American
diplomat put it - in the moment of political decision, only
the diplomat is authorized to commit his country.

The Role of Diplomats

After due credit is given to the international civil
servants who saw the need for the Conference and who took
the lead in its preparation, and to the experts who provided the documentation and the choice of solutions, there
still remain two fundamental questions. Who created the
framework in which the Conference could be established
and the climate in which it functioned? What forces made
it possible for one hundred nineteen nations to meet in a

spirit of conciliation, and who prevailed on their governments to participate?

The international civil servant might have written
an instructive book on the aims of developing countries;
pinpointing their needs and the aid which they had a right
to expect from the developed countries. The expert might
have used his knowledge in the academic field or for the
benefit of a government which asked his advice. But who
provided the forum on which these findings could be presented to the world and who assured the orderly and de-
corous character of the Conference proceedings?

Traditional diplomacy had been responsible for a long
series of meetings, conferences and congresses throughout the course of modern history. United Nations diplomacy was responsible for the establishment of the Conference on Trade and Development. United Nations diplomacy set a milestone in the economic evolution of the developing countries when - as one delegate from a newly
emerged nation in Africa so aptly put it - for the first time
the representatives of the people of Africa, Asia and Latin
America sat face to face with their former colonizers to
talk about economic matters.

Skillful diplomatic strategy was needed to bring together the representatives of nations which are at many
stages of development and have a wide variety of political,
economic and social systems; and to conduct discussions
between proponents of the conflicting interests of East and
West, North and South, whose deep-rooted ideological differences were thrown into relief during some of the Conference committee meetings. Representatives of United
Nations missions and related branches of United Nations
diplomacy achieved a balance of interests in a frank exchange of views which promised to bring benefits to all
concerned. It was the work of the diplomats which created
in patient and painstaking negotiations a climate of opinion favorable to the Conference.

The new diplomacy proved its professional ability
even by the high standards set by Nicolson[10]: "Diplomacy
. . . is not the art of conversation; it is the art of drafting precise instruments in ratifyable form." The General
Debate, during a series of Plenary Sessions, may not have
represented a diplomatic accomplishment; and indeed, the
participants in the debate were mostly political appointees,
heading various departments of member governments. The

work accomplished in the five committees, however, resulted in precise draft resolutions which could be ratified. Care-
ful scrutiny of committee work reveals the deft handling of
sensitive issues and continued striving for a compromise.
And it was the crowning feat of United Nations diplomacy
at the Conference that unanimous acceptance was achieved
in many instances, in spite of widely divergent views on
some of the subjects covered.

Moreover, a new development during the Conference
proved the dynamic quality of the new diplomacy. Although
the number of new and rapidly developing nations which
had joined the United Nations during the last few years
occupy a substantial portion of the earth, the balance of
power had not shifted since the Treaty of Versailles in
1919. In spite of the numerical strength of their vote in
the General Assembly, the developing nations were not
able to assert themselves diplomatically. Before the Conference, more or less futile attempts were made by certain regional and other groupings of developing countries
to make their influence felt. The Conference seemed to
offer an opportunity to change this state of affairs; and
indeed, when at the end of the Conference seventy-seven
underdeveloped nations submitted a Joint Declaration, a
landmark was set.

It remains to be seen whether the diplomatic align-
ment of the seventy-seven developing nations vis-a-vis
the developed nations will be used constructively; whether
the voting bloc which might be formed by these nations
will result in a power struggle, simply producing majori-
ties against the developed minority from which it expects
continued cooperation;[11] or whether diplomacy will be
able to take advantage of the new unity achieved at the Conference for the purpose of improving international relations, by using it as an instrument for persuasion and more
or less subtle pressure.

Present-day diplomats, faced with these new tasks,
need all the qualifications of traditional diplomacy. Most
governments feel that, in addition, specialized training in
a given profession should give the diplomat basic education in some of the fields of knowledge which shape international relations today. It is debatable whether such specialization will prove useful, however, and how far it
should go. The representative of a major Western power
pointed out that it is almost impossible nowadays for an

individual to acquire expertise in all the subjects which a
diplomatic representative has to deal with; but he added
that some degree of expertise in a diplomat engaged in
economic negotiations and conferences is very useful if
not essential, and that his own country seeks to ensure
that all diplomatic representatives acquire economic knowledge and experience. This expresses the opinion of all
delegates who answered the question about the specialized
training needed by diplomats. While fourteen answers
made it quite clear that the diplomat with some expert
knowledge will not replace the expert pure and simple but
will merely be better equipped to participate in negotiations
and will have the advantage of being able to better appreciate and evaluate the expert's advice given to him, one
member of the Preparatory Committee of the Conference
drew attention to the important fact that developing countries may face an added difficulty which affects their approach. The scarcity of personnel in developing countries
might create the need for diplomatic representatives who
are also experts; "economic diplomats", as some delegates called them in their replies to the questionnaire,
would have to serve in a double function until the developing
countries will have a sufficient number of trained experts
and diplomats available to allow a division of functions.
    It is hoped that this is a passing phase in their de-
velopment. As some representatives rightly pointed out,
diplomats are experts in their own field: they are experts
in the art of diplomacy; and specialist training should not
detract from the acquisition of experience in the diplomat's
main field of activity, namely the relations between governments.

Outlook

    The creation of new instruments for international re-
lations comes, as a rule, in answer to some immediate
need. Thus, regional arrangements in Europe, in Africa,
Asia and Latin America were designed to bring a measure
of economic unity and relief to groups of countries. Some
participants were content with agreements as a measure
for the solution of current problems in the specific field.
Others, however, viewed agreements as the nucleus of a
more comprehensive and universal grouping for which the
limited beginning was preparing the way.

A similar approach can be noticed among the participants of the United Nations Conference on Trade and Development. A question about the usefulness of the permanent machinery beyond its original economic purpose produced a positive reaction. Replies ranged from an em-
phatic affirmation by a representative of a Communist power
to the more guarded answer by a Western delegate. A
Latin American diplomat explained the reasoning behind
his own expectations: that he saw one of the great threats
of peace in the extremely unbalanced international economic situation and that, therefore, the removal of that
imbalance through UNCTAD might be a positive factor in
the political field.

This type of conclusion is based on the view that, as
a Belgian newspaper wrote, "It is a fact that on the international level, economic relations precede political relations". [12] But the article continues: "Instances are also
known where the opposite happened, when sometimes political decisions preceded and favored economic relations."

The problematic role of cause and effect in the connection between peace and economics is more clearly described in the reply given by a diplomat from a major Western power who expressed the thought that prosperity depends on peace probably to a greater extent than peace
depends on prosperity; and that it is not possible to carry
on economic activities in a political vacuum. As a result,
he felt that the usefulness of the new organization could
be fully realized only if it remained conscious of political
realities and if peace were preserved. It was his considered opinion that the main contribution must come from
the U.N. organization as a whole through the harmonious
working together of all its members.

To achieve this harmonious working together of all
nations is the continuing task of U.N. diplomacy; an illustration of its success is the United Nations Conference on
Trade and Development.

APPENDIX

QUESTIONNAIRE

SUBMITTED TO REPRESENTATIVES OF MEMBER STATES

---

1. Does the Conference on Trade and Development represent an accomplishment of International Diplomacy?

2. Do you consider international conferences more useful for the solution of economic problems than bilateral agreements?

3. During the course of the Conference, you had occasion to work with international civil servants and with experts. Do you feel that the diplomat's background and training enable him to make a contribution to international conferences which goes beyond the contribution made by those other two groups?
> a. What is the most valuable contribution a diplomat can make to international conferences?
> b. From your experience, what is the contribution of the civil servant?
> c. From your experience, what is the contribution of the expert?

4. Should international civil servants confine their activities to technical and administrative matters?

5. In your opinion, should experts sit at the conference table? Do you think it preferable to have experts act as advisers to diplomats?

6. Would you consider it useful to have diplomats trained in professions and techniques so that they themselves would be able to function as experts? If so, for what reasons?

7. In your personal judgement, did the Conference accomplish its purpose?

8. What do you think of the permanent machinery established by the Conference? Will it be merely one more international organization? Or will it add something new and different to the United Nations system?

9.   What do you think of the possibility that the new international machinery will be useful beyond its original economic purpose: that closer and more permanent international cooperation and division of labor will have its effect on the political level, and diminish the threat of war ?

NOTES

FOREWORD

1   Address of U Thant, reprinted in Addresses and
Public Statements 1957-1963: Towards World Peace (New
York: Thomas Yoseloff, 1964), p. 152.

CHAPTER 1

1   Ragnar Numelin, The Beginnings of Diplomacy: A
Sociological Study of Intertribal and International Relations (New York: Philosophical Library, 1950), pp. 291-
315.

2   Harold Nicolson, The Evolution of Diplomatic Method
(London: Constable & Co. Ltd., 1954), pp. 40-42.

3   Harold Nicolson, Diplomacy (London: Oxford University Press, Third Edition, 1963), p. 60.

4   Hedwig Fleischhacker, Die Staats-und Voelkerrecht-
lichen Grundlagen der Moskanischen Aussenpolitik, 14. -
17. Jahrhundert (Breslau: Verlag Priebatsche Buchhand-
lung, 1938), p. 50.

5   Jean Baillou et Pierre Pelletier, Les Affaires Etrangeres (Paris: Presses Universitaires de France, 1962),
p. 47.

6   What Harold Nicolson calls "The French Method" was
the theory and method of international negotiations, organized by Richelieu. See The Evolution of Diplomatic Method,
p. 72.

7   John Tilley and Stephen Gaselee, The Foreign Office
(London: G. P. Putnam Sons, Ltd., 1953), p. 1.

8   Herbert von Hindenburg, Das Auswaertige Amt im
Wandel der Zeiten (Frankfurt am Main: Societaetsverlag,
1932), p. 1.

9   Tilley, op. cit., p. 32.

10   Others may wage wars; you, lucky Austria, arrange

marriages.

11   Fleischhacker, op. cit., p. 50.

12   Nicolson, The Evolution of Diplomatic Method, p. 43.

13   Ibid., p. 58.

14   A term derived from the French word for "nursery".

15   Hindenburg, op. cit., p. 2.

16   Frederick L. Schuman, War and Diplomacy in the
French Republic (London: Whittlesey House, 1931), pp. 31ff.

17   Gordon A. Craig and Felix Gilbert (ed.), The Diplomats 1919-1939 (Princeton, N.J.: Princeton University
Press, 1953), pp. 123-124.

18   Art. II.

19   In spite of basic and factual differences in ideology
and execution between the American revolution and the rise
of Bolshevism, a striking parallel can be observed: Craig,
op. cit., p. 235, speaks of Trotsky's intention to discon-
tinue diplomatic relations as soon as the revolution was
accomplished. This was an attempt to disassociate the
new state from its former connections.

20   Warren Frederick Ilchman, Professional Diplomacy
in the United States 1779-1939 (Chicago: The University
of Chicago Press, 1961), p. 18.

21   Ibid., p. 23.

22   Graham H. Stuart, The Department of State (New
York: The MacMillan Company, 1949), p. 52.

23   Francis Wharton (ed.), The Revolutionary Diplomatic Correspondence of the United States (Washington,
1889), VI, p. 52, as quoted by Thomas A. Bailey, A Diplomatic History of the American People (New York: Ap-
pleton-Century-Crofts, Inc., Sixth Edition, 1958), p. 29.

24   Ibid. , p. 41.

25   Nicolson, The Evolution of Diplomatic Method, pp. 11-
13.

26   Democracy in America (London: Oxford University
Press, 1946), p. 161.

27   Ilchman, op. cit., p. 3.

28   Ibid. , p. 23.

29   Ibid. , p. 16.

30   Howard Wriggins, "Foreign Assistance and Political Development" in Development of the Emerging Countries (Washington: Brookings Institution, 1962), p. 193.

31   John Connel, "The Office": A Study of British Foreign Policy and its Makers, 1919-1951 (New York: St.
Martin's Press, 1958), p. 18.

32   Qualities of an ideal diplomacy, as enumerated by
Harold Nicolson, Diplomacy , p. 126.

33   Nicolson, in Diplomacy, p. 15, quoting the Oxford
English Dictionary.

34   Connel, op. cit., p. 25.

35   Craig and Gilbert, op. cit. , p. 679.

36   Connel, op. cit., p. 18.

37   After World War I, the few underdeveloped countries
which had attained independence, began to build up a foreign service, and the new nations, freed from colonialism
after World War II, followed the example of the great powers in the establishment of career diplomacy.

38   The Department of State 1963: A Report to the Citi-
zen (Department of State Publication 7530, General Foreign Policy Series 187, Released May, 1963), pp. 89-
91.

39   Craig and Gilbert, op. cit., p. 409.

40   Ibid., pp. 235-243.

41   The Old Diplomacy and the New, The David Davies
Memorial Institute of International Studies (London: Annual Memorial Lecture, March 19, 1961), p. 4.

42   Ibid., p. 4.

43   Diplomacy in the Nuclear Age (Cambridge, Mass.:
Harvard University Press, 1959), p. 8.

44   Ibid., p. 8.

45   Ibid., p. 11.

46   Compare Art. 99 of the U.N. Charter.

CHAPTER 2

1   The Thessalian League in ancient Greece for the first
time appointed an official who was directly responsible to
the League.

2   A survey on the "growth of the idea" of international
organization is included in L. Larry Leonard's International
Organization (New York: McGraw-Hill Book Company, Inc.,
1951), pp. 23-29.

3   Inis L. Claude, Jr., Swords into Plowshares: The Problems
Progress of International Organization (New York: Random House,
Third Edition, 1964), p. 21.

4   John G. Stoessinger, The Might of Nations: World
Politics in Our Time (New York: Random House, 1961),
p. 222.

5   Leonard, op. cit., lists on page 25 these interven-
tions.

6   Ibid., p. 25.

7   Joseph P. Chamberlain, International Organization
(New York: Carnegie Endowment of International Peace,
Second Printing, 1956), cites such cases on page 93.

8   The word "shall" was interpreted to be synonymous
with "may", which equalized the status of old and new agencies.

9   Woodrow Wilson considered this one of the essential
functions of the League. The Messages and Papers of
Woodrow Wilson, Vol. II, p. 985, as quoted by Leonard,
op. cit., p. 128.

10   As quoted by Leonard, op. cit., p. 479.

11   Ibid., pp. 36-37.

12   Kenneth W. Thompson, American Diplomacy and
Emergent Patterns (New York: New York University Press,
1962), p. 175.

13   Vera Micheles Dean, The Four Cornerstones of Peace
(New York: McGraw-Hill Book Company, 1946), p. xvi.

14   Leonard, op. cit., p. 44.

15   Ibid., p. 47; also Claude, op. cit., p. 61.

16   Dean, op. cit., p. 26.

17   Leonard, op. cit., p. 63.

18   On December 17, 1963, a Resolution was adopted by
the General Assembly which changes the representation
in the Security Council. Members have been requested
to ratify the Charter revision before September 1, 1965.
The Resolution provides for the enlargement from eleven
to fifteen members, of which ten will be nonpermanent.
The aim of that change is the more equitable representation of the different parts of the world in the nonpermanent membership. Decisions in procedural matters would
require an affirmative vote of any nine members; decisions in all other matters would require nine affirmative
votes, including those of the five permanent members. Is-

sues Before the Nineteenth General Assembly, International Conciliation Number 550 (New York: Carnegie Endowment for International Peace, November, 1964), pp. 41-43. The Resolution also introduces changes in the composition of the Economic and Social Council of the United Nations.

19   This follows the analysis by Stoessinger, op. cit., p. 248.

20   Claude, op. cit., p. 77.

21   The Constitutions of FAO, the Bank and the Fund became effective only in 1945.

22   The Arab League consists of the U.A.R. (Egypt), Algeria, Iraq, Jordan, Kuwait, Lebanon, Lybia, Morocco, Saudi Arabia, Sudan, Syria, Tunis and Yemen.

23   Claude, op. cit., p. 242.

24   Members of NATO are: the United States, Canada, Belgium, Denmark, France, Greece, Great Britain, Iceland, Italy, Luxemburg, Netherlands, Norway, Portugal, Turkey, West Germany.

25   The ANZUS countries, Pakistan, the Philippines and Thailand joined with Great Britain and France in SEATO.

26   CENTO, combining Britain, Iran, Turkey and Pakistan, is the successor to the Baghdad Pact.

27   The Conference of European Powers for the Assurance of Peace and Security in Europe.

28   See the analysis by Stoessinger, op. cit., p. 9.

29   Ibid., p. 314.

30   G. F. Deniau, The Common Market (New York: Frederick A. Praeger, 1960), p. 6.

31   Belgium, Denmark, France, Ireland, Italy, Luxemburg, Poland, Norway, Sweden and Britain.

CHAPTER 3

1   Barbara Ward, The Rich Nations and the Poor Nations   (New York: W. W. Norton & Company, Inc., 1962),
p. 38, estimates that 80% of mankind belongs to the poor
nations.

2   Robert Theobald, The Rich and the Poor   (New York:
Clarkson N. Potter, Inc., 1960), p. 28.

3   Ibid., pp. 86-110.

4   Compare Ward, op. cit., p. 91, and Theobald, op. cit.,
        p. 65.

5   H. W. Singer, International Development: Growth and
Change   (New York: McGraw-Hill Book Company, 1964),
p. 20.

6   Ward, op. cit., p. 59.

7   For the causes of underdevelopment, compare Ever-
ett E. Hagen, "A Framework for Analyzing Economic and
Political Change", Development of the Emerging Countries:
An Agenda for Research (Washington, D. C.: Brookings
Institution, 1962), pp. 24-25; Vera Micheles Dean, West
and Non-West: New Perspectives (New York: Holt, Rinehart and Winston, Inc., 1963), p. 105; Ward, op. cit.,
pp. 38-56.

8   Measures for the Economic Development of Underdeveloped Countries. Report by a Group of Experts, appointed by the Secretary General of the United Nations,
Department of Economic Affairs, New York, May, 1951
(E/1986, St/ECA/10), p. iv.

9   R.S. Eckaus, "Technological Change in the Less Developed Areas", Development of the Emerging Countries,
p. 134.

10   This particular type of problem was one of the issues
discussed at the U.N. Conference on Trade and Development.

11   Trade Blocs and Common Markets (New York: Alfred

A. Knopf, 1963), pp. 235-241.

12   Hagen, op. cit., pp. 11-26.

13   Gerhard Colm and Theodor Geiger, "Country Pro-graming as a Guide to Development", in Development of the Emerging Countries , pp. 45-52, define the steps in economic planning.

14   Jan Tinbergen, Shaping the World Economy: Sug-gestions for an International Economic Policy (New York: The Twentieth Century Fund, 1962), pp. 11-12.

15   Arthur T. Mosher, "Research on Rural Problems" in Development of the Emerging Countries, pp. 86-87.

16   Pierre Moussa, The Underprivileged Nations (Bos-ton, Mass.: Beacon Press, 1959), p. 78, draws attention to the fact that the temptation to use surplus income for consumption instead of saving is also a result of poverty, because of the desire to raise the low standard of living.

17   For "Methods by Which to Explore, Appraise and Stimulate Private Investment", compare Jan Tinbergen, The Design of Development (Baltimore, Md.: The Johns Hopkins Press, 1958), pp. 46-69.

18   Measures for the Economic Development of Under-developed Countries, pp. 35-44.

19   Ibid., p. 71.

20   Ibid., p. 72.

21   Tinbergen, Shaping the World Economy, p. 41.

22   Compare a speech by Secretary of State Dulles, in April, 1955, quoted by Jack N. Behrman and Wilson E. Schmidt, International Economics (New York: Rinehart & Company, 1957), p. 401.

23   Eugene R. Black, The Diplomacy of Economic De-velopment (Cambridge, Mass.: Harvard University Press, 1960), p. 45.

24   Ibid., pp. 21-22.

25   Ibid., p. 24.

26   Tinbergen, Shaping the World Economy, p. 29.

27   Statistical Abstract of the United States, 1963 (Washington, D.C.: Bureau of the Census, 1963), pp. 858-859.

28   Tinbergen, Shaping the World Economy, pp. 26-27.

29   Black, op. cit., pp. 23-24.

30   Tinbergen, Shaping the World Economy, pp. 27-28.

31   Ward, op. cit., p. 128.

32   The ideological background and the reasoning behind this approach is analyzed in The Ideologies of the Developing Nations, Paul H. Sigmund, Jr., ed. (New York: Frederick A. Praeger, 1963), pp. 11-22.

33   Klaus E. Knorr, Ruble Diplomacy: Challenge to American Foreign Aid (Princeton, N.J.: Center of International Studies, 1956), p. 12.

34   Compare also Joseph S. Berliner, Soviet Economic Aid: The New Aid and Trade Policy in Underdeveloped Countries (New York: Frederick A. Praeger, 1958), p. 1.

35   Julius Stulman, World Economic Development: A Program for Utilization of Full Capacity Production (Washington, D.C.: Public Affairs Press, 1961), p. 15.

36   Stoessinger, op. cit., p. 199.

37   Robert Loring Allen, Soviet Economic Warfare (Washington, D.C.: Public Affairs Press, 1960), p. 42.

38   Tinbergen, Shaping the World Economy, pp. 36-39.

CHAPTER 4

1   In 1920, an Economic Commission and a Financial
Commission were established which met three to four times
a year.

2   The United Nations and Economic and Social Cooperation, by Robert Asher, et al. (Washington, D.C.: The
Brookings Institution, 1957), p. 10.

3   G. Van der Veen, Aiding Underdeveloped Countries
through International Economic Cooperation (Delft: Naam-
loze Vennootschap W.D. Meinema, 1954), p. 67.

4   Ibid., p. 66.

5   The United Nations and Economic and Social Cooperation, p. 12.

6   The validity of these and other critical observations
was demonstrated during the League's futile attempt to
impose economic sanctions on Italy during the invasion
of Abyssinia.

7   The United Nations and Economic and Social Cooperation, p. 27.

8   Van der Veen, op. cit., p. 64.

9   Stoessinger, op. cit., p. 258.

10   Van der Veen, op. cit., p. 69.

11   Issues Before the Nineteenth General Assembly, p. 42.

12   Frank N. Trager, "Economic Matters", Annual Review of United Nations Affairs 1954 (New York: New York
University Press, 1955), p. 33.

13   The United Nations and Economic and Social Cooperation, p. 440.

14   Stoessinger, op. cit., p. 260.

15   Black, op. cit., p. 67.

16   Tinbergen, Shaping the World Economy, p. 226.

17   Ibid., p. 29.

18   Alvin Z. Rubinstein, The Soviets in International Organizations: Changing Policy Toward Developing Countries, 1953-1963
(Princeton, N.J.: Princeton University Press, 1964), p. 48.

19   Stoessinger, op. cit., p. 382.

20   Tinbergen, Shaping the World Economy, pp. 40-45.

21   For the position taken by the U.S.S.R. on this matter,
compare the chapter "Moscow and Technical Assistance" in
Rubinstein, op. cit., pp. 32-89.

22   Alvin Z. Rubinstein, "Soviet and American Policies
in International Economic Organizations", International
Organizations, Vol. XVIII, No. 1 (Winter, 1964), pp. 29-52.

23   David Owen, "A Decade for Development", Annual
Review of United Nations Affairs, 1961-1962 (New York:
New York University Press, 1963), pp. 81-101.

24   The Conference on the Problems of Economic Development (Cairo, U.A.R.: General Organization for Government
Printing Offices, 1962).

25   General Assembly Resolution 1707 (XVI).

26   General Assembly Resolution 1710 (XVI).

27   ECOSOC Resolution 917 (XXXIV).

28   An illustration of this broad approach is the proposal
of the Soviet delegation to include in the agenda a study of
the interrelationship between general disarmament and
world trade.

29   Interim Report of the Preparatory Committee, ECOSOC,
Official Records, Doc. E/3320, XXXV.

30   ECOSOC Resolution 944 (XXXV).

31   ECOSOC Resolution 943 (XXXV).

32   ECOSOC Resolution 919 (XXXIV).

33   ECOSOC Resolution 963 (XXXVI).

34   Towards a New Trade Policy for Development: Report
by the Secretary General of the United Nations Conference
on Trade and Development (United Nations Publications,
Sales No. 64. II. B. 4), Introduction.

35   Ibid., Preface.

36   Draft of the Interim Report To Be Submitted to the
Economic and Social Council. Preparatory Committee,
First Session, February 1, 1963, E/Conf. 46/PC/L. 11/
Add. 1.

CHAPTER 5

1   Abdel Moneim El-Kaissouni of U. A. R., President
of the Conference, E/Conf. 46/Sta./3.

2   Final Act of the United Nations Conference on Trade
and Development, E/Conf. 46/L. 28, p. 6.

3   E/Conf. 46/ Sta./1.

4   E/Conf. 46/ Sta./3.

5   E/Conf. 46/Sta./4/Corr. 1.

6   E/Conf. 46/Sta./9.

7   Raphael Saller, Minister of Finance, Economic Affairs and Planning of the Ivory Coast, E/Conf. 46/Sta./18.

8   Bachir Moumaza, Minister of National Economy of
Algeria, E/Conf. 46/Sta./110.

9   Zanna Bukar Dipcharima, Federal Minister of Commerce and Industry of the Federal Republic of Nigeria,
E/Conf. 46/Sta./37.

10   Compare the statement of Joao Augusto de Araujo Cas-

tro, Minister of State of External Relations of Brazil, that
for the first time in the history of economic conferences,
underdeveloped countries had come here as a "united front".
E/Conf. 46/Sta./7.

11   This point was particularly mentioned by Roberto
Jordan Pando, Minister of Planning and Coordination of
Bolivia, E/Conf. 46/Sta./56, and by L. Marconi Robin-
son, Minister of Agriculture, Industry and Commerce of
Trinidad and Tobago, E/Conf. 46/Sta./108.

12   For instance the delegations of Albania, Bulgaria,
Cuba, Guinea, Indonesia, Roumania, the U.S.S.R.

13   Delegations which did not wish to see GATT continued
were from Bolivia, Bulgaria, Byelorussia, Cyprus, Czechoslovakia, Ghana, Guinea, Mongolia, Poland, Syria and the
U.S.S.R.

14   Lincoln Steel, President of the International Chamber
of Commerce, E/Conf. 46/Sta./114.

15   N. Diederichs, Minister of Foreign Affairs of South
Africa, E/Conf. 46/Sta./114.

16   Compare the statements by the delegates from Af-
ghanistan, Ceylon, India, Iran, Korea, Liberia, Philippines, Sierra Leone, Sweden, Thailand, Trinidad and the
United Kingdom of Great Britain and Northern Ireland.

17   For instance Iran.

18   Kiichi Migazawa, Minister of the State of Japan,
asked that every effort be made to avoid the concentration
of world trade through the practice of regionalism. E/
Conf. 46/Sta./57. Kasem Sriphayak, Minister of Economic Affairs of Thailand, urged that industrialized regional
economic groupings be not allowed to affect adversely the
welfare of third countries. E/Conf. 46/Sta./75. Kico
Ngjela, Minister of Trade of Albania, directed his opposition to a specific regional body, namely the European
Common Market, describing it as a serious obstacle to
international trade. E/Conf. 46/Sta./66.

19   Ali Alikhani, Iran's Minister of Economy, E/Conf. 46/
Sta./85; Gehoash Sibakyalwayo Mayanga Nkangi, Minister
of Commerce of Uganda, E/Conf. 46/Sta./88; Rudolph
Yav, Minister of External Trade of Congo (Leopoldville),
E/Conf. 46/Sta./97; and Adam Malik, Minister of Trade,
Indonesia, E/Conf. 46/Sta./98, expressed their govern-
ments' concern over these developments.

20   Federal Councillor Hans Schaffner, E/Conf. 46/Sta./
       20.

21   Dr. Bruno Kreisky, Minister of Foreign Affairs of
Austria, E/Conf. 46/Sta./24.

22   George W. Ball, Under Secretary of State, E/Conf.
46/Sta./14.

23   R. C. Lightbourne, Minister of Commerce and Industry, E/Conf. 46/Sta./44.

24   Cornelio Balmaceda, Secretary of Commerce and
Industry, E/Conf. 46/Sta./103.

25   Vu Vanmau, Ambassador of the Republic of Viet
Nam in London, E/Conf. 46/Sta./68.

26   Maurice Brasseur, Minister of Foreign Trade and
Technical Assistance, E/Conf. 46/Sta./6.

27   Edward Heath, Secretary of State of Industry, E/
Conf. 46/Sta./92.

28   Courmo Barcougni, Minister of Finance and Economic Affairs, E/Conf. 46/Sta./87.

29   The President of the Conference decided that the issue of compensatory financing should be split between the
First and the Third Committees. The need for compensatory financing and its general aspects to be treated by the
First, the technical aspects by the Third Committee.

30   E/Conf. 46/8.1/SR.1-70.

31   E/Conf. 46/131.

32   E/Conf. 46/C. 2/SR. 1-62.

33   E/Conf. 46/132.

34   E/Conf. 46/132, p. 7.

35   Ibid., p. 21.

36   The First Committee dealt with the general aspects of compensatory financing.

37   E/Conf. 46/133.

38   E/Conf. 46/S. 2/SR. 1-64.

39   E/Conf. 46/133, p. 27.

40   Ibid., p. 94.

41   E/Conf. 46/134 and Add. 1.

42   E/Conf. 46/50.

43   E/Conf. 46/51.

44   E/Conf. 46/134, p. 3.

45   E/Conf. 46/C. 5/SR. 1-46.

46   The first of these principles stated the basic precept; "The recognition of the right of each land-locked state of free access to the sea is an essential principle for the expansion of international trade and economic development.

47   Problems of landlocked countries, such as their need for adequate transit facilities, had been recognized by the United Nations General Assembly Resolution 1028 (XI) and by the ECAFE Ministerial Conference of 1963 on Asian Economic Cooperation as well as by the ECAFE Resolution 51 (XX).

48   E/Conf. 46/135.

49   E/Conf. 46/L. 28.

50   Proposals of the General Committee Regarding the Final Act, Report and Record of Proceedings of the Conference, E/Conf. 46/110.

51   Ibid., p. 1.

52   Ibid., p. 3.

53   E/Conf. 46/L. 28, Final Clauses, pp. 2-10.

54   E/Conf. 46/L. 28/Add. 1.

55   E/Conf. 46/139.

56   E/Conf. 46/SR. 36.

57   ECOSOC Resolution 1011 (XXXVII).

CHAPTER 6

1   Supra, pp. 98-99.

2   E/Conf. 46/132, p. 14.

3   Supra, p. 91, n. 10.

4   E/Conf. 46/L. 28/Add. 1, p. 18.

5   E/Conf. 46/L. 28, Annex B, p. 10.

6   Ibid., p. 36.

7   E/Conf. 46/Sta./122.

8   This was, for instance, the opinion stated by the delegate from Brazil who saw in GATT "inborn defects and sins inherent". E/Conf. 46/Sta./7.

9   For an analysis of the aims pursued by the Kennedy Round and the importance for developing countries, compare Miriam Camps, "The Kennedy Round", The World

Today, Vol. XX, No. 5 (May, 1964), pp. 215-223; G. Griffith Johnson, "A Perspective on the United Nations Conference on Trade and Development", The Department of State Bulletin, Vol. L, No. 1290 (March 16, 1964), pp. 410-415.

10   E/Conf. 46/134, p. 5.

11   The details of the debate in the Fourth Committee have been discussed, supra, pp. 102-104.

12   E/Conf. 46/L. 22 and Corr. 1.

13   E/Conf. 46/L. 28, Annex A, V. 1.

14   Ibid., Annex B, p. 13.

15   Ibid., pp. 6-7.

16   E/Conf. 46/L. 28, Annex A, p. 129.

17   Ibid., Annex A, pp. 136-139.

18   Ibid., Annex B, p. 13.

19   Dr. Raul Prebisch has been appointed.

20   E/Conf. 46/L. 28, Annex B, pp. 6-7.

21   Ibid., Annex B, p. 15.

22   Ibid., Annex B, p. 50.

23   Dr. Raul Prebisch, in an article on the "Spirit of Conciliation", U.N. Monthly Chronicle, United Nations Office for Public Information, Vol. 1, No. 3 (July, 1964), p. 75, pointed out that "the main difficulty that arose in this respect /conciliation machinery/ was the question of voting in the organs of the proposed new machinery. All groupings of nations at Geneva attached singular importance to this particular matter and therefore, certain aspects pertaining to it were left to the decision of the General Assembly."

24   A/5749, p. 4.

25   Ibid., p. 5.

26   E/Conf. 46/L.28, Annex B, p. 20.

27   Ibid., p. 45.

28   Ibid., p. 27.

29   Ibid., p. 56.

30   A/5749, Annex II.

31   Ibid., Annex I.

32   A./L. 449.

CHAPTER VII

1   E/Conf. 46/L.28/Add. 1.

2   E/Conf. 46/L.28.

3   U.N. Office of Public Information, United Nations
Conference on Trade and Development, Geneva, 23 March -
16 June, 1964.

4   Included in the Appendix.

5   Argentina, Chile, Colombia, Czechoslovakia, France,
India, Kenya, Lebanon, New Zealand, Pakistan, Senegal,
Tanzania, the Union of Soviet Socialist Republics, the Uni-
ted Arab Republic, the United Kingdom of Great Britain
and Northern Ireland, the United States of America, and
Yugoslavia.

6   The inauspicious beginning of Conference preparations is illustrated by a report of the New York Times News
Service of March 22, 1964, which started as follows: "Official Washington views the forthcoming U.N. Conference
on Trade and Development with about the same enthusiasm
as it views the approach of the hay fever season."

At the close of the Conference, Dr. Prebisch referred to another grim prediction: "The tower of Babel was an image much resorted to, and it was predicted that there would be a multiplicity of incoherent resolutions adopted in disorderly fashion. ..." E/Conf. 46/140, p. 13.

7   E/Conf. 46/Sta./3.

8   A/L. 449, p. 11.

9   Of these twelve experts, five were diplomats, who also participated in the Conference as members of delegations; four came from academic life; one was an international civil servant; and two held government positions.

10   Supra, p. 21.

11   Richard H. Gardner, In Pursuit of World Order: U.S. Foreign Policy and International Organizations (New York: Frederick A. Praeger, 1964), p. 170.

12   Le Soir, Brussels, April 30, 1964.

BIBLIOGRAPHY

I. PUBLIC DOCUMENTS

    1. United Nations Publications

United Nations Conference on Trade and Development.
        Provisional Agenda. E/CONF. 46/1.

--------. Summary Records of the Thirty-Six Plenary
         Meetings. E/CONF. 46/SR. 1-36.

--------. Reports of the Five Committees. E/CONF. 46/
         131-135.

--------. Final Act. E/CONF. 46/L. 28.

--------. Report. E/CONF. 46/L. 28/Add. 1.

--------. Report to the Secretary General: The Significance
         of the United Nations Conference on Trade and
         Development. E/CONF. 46/140.

--------. I. A Review of Action Taken by the Conference -
         II. An Appraisal of its Impact on Public Opinion.
         UN Office of Public Information, July, 1964.

--------. Press Kit. UN Office of Public Information, 1964.

--------. Proceedings. E/CONF. 46/141, Vols. I-VIII.

United Nations General Assembly. Report of the United
        Nations Conference on Trade and Development.
        Proposals Designed to Establish a Process of
        Conciliation within the United Nations Confer-
        ence on Trade and Development. A/5749.

--------. Report of the United Nations Conference on Trade
         and Development. Establishment of the United
         Nations Conference on Trade and Development as
         an Organ of the General Assembly: Draft Reso-
         lution submitted by the President of the General
         Assembly. A/L. 449.

United Nations Economic and Social Council. Interim Report
        of the Preparatory Committee of the United Na-
        tions Conference on Trade and Development (first

session). E/3720. Thirty-Fifth Session, New
York, 1963.

--------. Report of the Preparatory Committee of the United Nations Conference on Trade and Development (second session). E/3799. Thirty-sixth
Session, Geneva, 1963.

--------. Commodity and Trade Problems of Developing
Countries: Institutional Arrangements. Report
of the Group of Experts Appointed Under Economic and Social Council Resolution 919. Thirty-Sixth Session, Geneva, 1963.

--------. Statement by the Secretary General at the Opening of the General Debate on the World Economic
Situation at the Thirty-Seventh Session of the
Economic and Social Council, Geneva. ECOSOC/
2059.

United Nations Department of Economic Affairs.
Measures for the Economic Development of Under-Developed Countries: Report by a Group of
Experts appointed by the Secretary General of
the United Nations. E/1986, 3 May, 1951.

--------. The United Nations Development Decade: Proposals for Action. Report of the Secretary General. E/3613, 1962.

United Nations. Towards a New Trade Policy for Development. Report of the Secretary General of the
United Nations Conference on Trade and Development. E/CONF. 46/3, 1964.

--------. Monthly Chronicle. "Spirit of Conciliation" by
Raul Prebisch. Vol. 1, Number 3 (July, 1964).

2. Other Publications

General Agreement on Tariffs and Trade. The Role of
GATT in Relation to Trade and Development.
The Contracting Parties to the General Agree-

ment on Tariffs and Trade, Geneva, March 1964.

United Arab Republic. The Conference on Problems of
      Economic Development. General Organization
      for Government Printing Offices, Cairo, 1962.

II. BOOKS

Allen, Robert Loring. Soviet Economic Warfare. Wash-
      ington, D.C.: Public Affairs Press, 1960.

Arnold, H.J.P. Aid for Developing Countries: A Compara-
      tive Study. London: The Bodley Head, 1962.

Asher, Robert, et al. Development of the Emerging Coun-
      tries: An Agenda for Research. Washington,
      D.C.: The Brookings Institution, 1962.

--------. The United Nations and Economic and Social
      Co-operation. Washington, D.C.: The Brook-
      ings Institution, 1957.

Bailey, Sydney D. The Secretariat of the United Nations.
      United Nations Study Number 11. New York:
      Carnegie Endowment for International Peace, 1962.

Baillou, Jean, et Pelletier, Pierre. Les Affaires Etrangeres.
      Paris: Presses Universitaires de France, 1962.

Balandier, G.   Les Pays Sous-Developpee: Aspects et
      Perspectives. Paris: Les Cours de Droit, 1959.

Balogh, T.   Some Aspects of Economic Growth of Under-
      developed Areas. Three Lectures. New Delhi:
      National Council of Applied Economic Research,
      1961.

Barker, Josef (ed.). Foreign Aid and the National Interest.
      A Report on the Views of Leading Citizens in
      Twenty-Five Cities. New York: Council on For-
      eign Relations, 1952.

Bauer, Peter Tomas, and Yamey, B.S. The Economics
    of Underdeveloped Countries. Chicago: Chi-
    cago University Press, 1957.

Behrman, Jack N., and Schmidt, Wilson E. International
    Economics: Theory-Practice-Policy. New York:
    Rinehart & Company, Inc., 1957.

Benham, Frederick Charles. Economic Aid to Underdeve-
    loped Countries. London: Oxford University
    Press, 1961.

Benoit, Emile. Europe at Sixes and Sevens. New York:
    Columbia University Press, 1961.

Berliner, Joseph S. Soviet Economic Aid: The New Aid
    and Trade Policy in Underdeveloped Countries.
    New York: Council on Foreign Relations, 1958.

Black, Eugene R. The Diplomacy of Economic Develop-
    ment. Cambridge, Mass.: Harvard University
    Press, 1960.

Brand, W. The Struggle for a Higher Standard of Living:
    The Problem of the Underdeveloped Countries.
    Glencoe, Ill.: The Free Press, 1958.

Chamberlain, Joseph P. International Organization. New
    York: Carnegie Endowment for International
    Peace, Second Printing, 1956.

Claude, Inis L., Jr. Swords into Plowshares: The Prob-
    lems and Progress of International Organiza-
    tion. New York: Random House, Third Edi-
    tion, 1964.

Cleveland, Harlan. The Theory and Practice of Foreign
    Aid. A Paper Prepared for the Special Studies
    Project of the Rockefeller Brothers' Fund. Sy-
    racuse: 1956.

Connel, John. The "Office": A Study of British Foreign
    Policy and its Makers, 1919-1951. New York:
    St. Martin's Press, 1958.

Craig, Gordon A. and Gilbert, Felix (ed.). The Diplo-
          mats 1919-1939. Princeton, N. J. : Princeton
          University Press, 1953.

Dean, Vera Micheles. Builders of Emerging Nations. New
          York: Holt, Rinehart and Winston, 1961.

--------. The Four Cornerstones of Peace. New York:
          McGraw-Hill Book Company, Inc. ,1946.

--------. The Nature of the Non-Western World. New
          York: The New American Library, 1957.

Dean, Vera Micheles and Harootunian, Harry D. (ed.).
          West and Non-West: New Perspectives. New
          York: Holt, Rinehart and Winston, 1963.

Dell, Sidney. Trade Blocs and Common Markets. New
          York: Alfred A. Knopf, 1963.

Deniau, J. F. The Common Market: Its Structure and Pur-
          pose. New York: Frederick A. Praeger, 1960.

Fischer, M. Problemes Internationaux Relatifs aux Pays
          Sous-Devellopes. Paris: Association des Etudes
          Internationales, 1954-1955.

Gardner, Richard N. In Pursuit of World Order: U.S. For-
          eign Policy and International Organizations. New
          York: Frederick A. Praeger, 1964.

Hoffman, Paul G. The Greatest Challenge of All. New York:
          Public Affairs Committee, 1961.

Hunt, Gaillard. The Department of State of the United
          States: Its History and Functions. New Haven,
          Conn.: Yale University Press, 1964.

Ibrahim, Mohamed Fuad. The European Economic Commu-
          nity. Cairo: Egyptian General Finance Associa-
          tion, 1959. In Arabic.

Ilchman, Warren Frederick. Professional Diplomacy in
          the United States 1779 - 1939: A Study in Ad-

ministrative History. Chicago: The University
of Chicago Press, 1961.

Isard, Walter and Cumberland, John H. (ed.). Regional
Economic Planning: Techniques of Analysis for
Less Developed Areas. Paris: European Productivity Agency of the Organization for European Economic Co-operation, 1961.

Knorr, Klaus Eugen. Ruble Diplomacy: Challenge to American Foreign Aid. Princeton, N.J.: Center of
International Studies, 1956.

Krause, Walter. Economic Development: The Underdeveloped World and the American Interest. San
Francisco, Cal.: Wadsworth, 1961.

Leonard, L. Larry. International Organization. New York:
McGraw-Hill Book Company, Inc., 1951.

Lubrano-Lavadera, Eugene Michel. L'ours dans la Bergerie:
La Penetration Sovietique dans les Pays Sous-
Developpes. Paris: Berger-Levrault, 1960.

Madan, B.K. Economic Problems of Underdeveloped Countries in Asia. New Delhi: Indian Council of
World Affairs, 1953.

McCamy, James L. Conduct of the New Diplomacy. New
York: Harper & Row, 1964.

Mejira-Ricart, Marcio A. Crisis of Small States in the
Present Economic World: A Study of the Prob-
lems of Small Underdeveloped States. With
Special Reference to Central America and the
Caribbean Area. London: Farm Intelligence,
Ltd., 1960.

Moussa, Pierre. The Underprivileged Nations. Boston,
Mass.: Beacon Press, 1959.

Nicolson, Harold. Diplomacy. London: Oxford University Press, Third Edition, 1963.

--------. The Evolution of Diplomatic Method. London:
    Constable & Co. Ltd., 1954.

--------. The Old Diplomacy and the New. The David Da-
    vies Memorial Institute of International Studies.
    London: Annual Memorial Lecture, March,1961.

Numelin, Ragnar. The Beginnings of Diplomacy. A Socio-
    logical Study of Intertribal and International Re-
    lations. New York: Philosophical Library, 1950.

Pearson, Lester B. Diplomacy in the Nuclear Age. Cam-
    bridge, Mass.: Harvard University Press, 1959.

Perkins, Dexter. The American Approach to Foreign Pol-
    icy. Cambridge, Mass.: Harvard University
    Press, 1955.

Rondot, Pierre. The Changing Patterns of the Middle East.
    New York: Frederick A. Praeger, 1962.

Rosser, Richard Franklin. The Soviet Union and the Under-
    developed Countries in the United Nations. Ann
    Arbor, Mich.: University Microfilms, 1962.

Rubinstein, Alvin Z. The Soviets in International Organiza-
    tions: Changing Policy Toward Developing Coun-
    tries, 1953 - 1963. Princeton, N.J.: Princeton
    University Press, 1964.

Schuman, Frederick L. War and Diplomacy in the French
    Republic. London: Whittlesey House, 1931.

Scott, John. Democracy is not Enough: A Personal Survey
    of the Hungry World. New York: Harcourt,
    Brace & Co., 1960.

Seabury, Paul. The Wilhelmstrasse: A Study of German
    Diplomats under the Nazi Regime. Berkeley,
    Calif.: University of California Press, 1954.

Shukeir, Mohamed Labib. Economic International Rela-
    tions. Cairo: El-Nahda, Second Edition, 1958.
    In Arabic.

Sigmund, Paul E., Jr. (ed.). The Ideologies of the De-
        veloping Nations. New York: Frederick A.
        Praeger, Third Printing, 1963.

Singer, H. W. International Development: Growth and
        Change. New York: McGraw Hill Book Com-
        pany, 1964.

Stanford Research Institute, Stanford University, Interna-
        tional Industrial Development Center. The For-
        eign Deficit of the United States: Causes and Is-
        sues. A Staff Study. Menlo Park, Calif: Wil-
        liam B. Dale, 1960.

Stoessinger, John C. The Might of Nations: World Politics in
        Our Time. New York: Random House. 1961.

Stuart, Graham E. The Department of State: A History of its
        Organization, Procedure and Personnel. New York:
        The MacMillan Company, 1949.

Stulman, Julius. World Economic Development: A Program
        for Utilization of Full Capacity Production. Wash-
        ington, D. C.: Public Affairs Press, 1961.

Theobald, Robert. The Rich and the Poor. New York:
        Clarkson N. Potter, Inc., 1960.

Thompson, Kenneth W. American Diplomacy and Emergent
        Patterns. New York: New York University Press,
        1962.

Tilley, John and Gaselee, Stephen. The Foreign Office.
        London: G. P. Putnam Sons, Ltd., 1953.

Tinbergen, Jan. The Design of Development. Baltimore,
        Md.: The Johns Hopkins Press, 1958.

--------. Shaping the World Economy: Suggestions for an
        International Economic Policy. New York: The
        Twentieth Century Fund, 1962.

U Thant. Toward World Peace: Speeches and Public State-
        ments. Selected by Jacob Baal Teshuva. New

York: Thomas Yoseloff, 1964.

Van der Veen, G. Aiding Underdeveloped Countries Through
        International Economic Cooperation. Delft:
        Naamloze Venneetschap W. D. Meinema, 1954.

Ward, Barbara. The Rich Nations and the Poor Nations.
        New York: W. W. Norton & Co. , 1962.

Wiggins, James W. (ed.). Foreign Aid Reexamined: A
        Critical Appraisal. Washington, D. C.: Public
        Affairs Press, 1958.

III. PAMPHLETS

Boutros-Ghali, B. Y. The Arab League 1945 - 1955. In-
        ternational Conciliation No. 498. New York:
        Carnegie Endowment for International Peace,
        May, 1954.

Issues Before the Nineteenth General Assembly. Interna-
        tional Conciliation No. 550. New York: Car-
        negie Endowment for International Peace, No-
        vember, 1964.

Korbonski, Andrzej. COMECON. International Concilia-
        tion No. 549. New York: Carnegie Endowment
        for International Peace, September, 1964.

Stern, Robert M. Policies for Trade and Development.
        International Conciliation No. 548. New York:
        Carnegie Endowment for International Peace,
        May, 1964.

Wionczek, Miguel S. Latin American Free Trade Associa-
        tion. International Conciliation No. 551. New
        York: Carnegie Endowment for International
        Peace, January, 1965.

IV. ARTICLES AND PERIODICALS

Camps, Miriam. "The Kennedy Round", The World Today,

Vol. 30, No. 5 (May 1964), pp. 215 - 223.

Foreign Affairs. 1963 - 1964.

Hovet, Thomas, Jr. "United Nations Diplomacy", Journal
    of International Affairs, Vol. XVII, No. 1 (1963)
    pp. 29 - 41.

International Organization. 1964.

Shonfield, Andrew. "Trade as a Tool of Development: The
    Issues at Geneva", International Affairs, Vol.
    40, No. 2 (April 1964), pp. 219 - 231.

INDEX

ANZUS, 42
Arab League, 42

Balance of power, 8, 11, 14, 26, 134
BENELUX, 44
Bretton Woods Conference, 40, 71
Bruce Report, 66, 69

Cairo Conference, 77
Central Treaty Organization (CENTO), 43
Collective security, 42
Common Market, 45-47, 52
Conciliation, 30, 120, 123, 131
Congress of Vienna, 8, 14, 25-27, 30, 69
Consular service, 6, 9
Council for Mutual Economic Assistance (COMECON), 42
Council of Europe, 46

Diplomacy, definition of, 16, 21, 133
Diplomatic service, 6, 7, 9, 10, 11, 13, 14
Dumbarton Oaks Conference, 34, 35, 69

EURATOM, 45
European Coal and Steel Community, 44-45
European Economic Community, See Common Market
European Free Trade Organization, 46
Experts, 22, 30, 35, 56, 66, 71, 74, 82-83, 95, 98,
    131-132, 135

Food and Agricultural Organization (FAO), 40, 73, 95, 98
Foreign Office, 6, 7, 9, 10, 14
Foreign Service, 6, 9, 14, 19

General Agreement on Tariffs and Trade (GATT), 72-73,
    76, 78, 82, 85, 91-92, 102, 103, 112-115

Hague Peace Conferences, 26, 32
Hot Springs Conference, 40, 73

International Bank for Reconstruction and Development
    (Bank), 40, 71, 103
International Civil Aviation Organization, 71
International civil service (servants), 22, 30, 39, 128,
    129-131, 133
International Development Corporation, 72, 76

International Finance Corporation, 72
International Labor Organization (ILO), 40, 66, 67
International machinery for industrial development, 103, 110-111
International Maritime Consultative Organization, 71
International Metereological Organization, 28
International Monetary Fund (Fund), 40, 72, 103
International Telegraph Union, 27, 28, 67, 71
International Trade Organization, 72, 82, 102, 129
Italian influence, 3-5

Kennedy Round, 114

Landlocked countries, 104-105
Latin American Free Trade Organization (LAFTA), 47
League of Nations, 22, 28-33, 34, 36, 38, 39, 65-68, 74, 131
    Assembly, 31
    Council, 31
    Covenant, 30, 31, 32, 65
    Economic and Financial Organization, 66, 74
    Permanent Court of International Justice, 31, 38
    Secretariat, 29-30
    Secretary General, 29

Marshall Plan, 44, 57-58, 59

National income, 48, 49, 56
North Atlantic Treaty Organization (NATO), 42

Organization of American States (OAS), 41
Organization for African Unity (OAU), 42
Organization for European Economic Cooperation. See Marshall Plan

Pan-American Union, 41
Pan-European Congress, 46
Permanent missions, 5, 6
Personal diplomacy, 7, 8, 20-22
Planning, 54, 60-61
Public opinion, 4, 6, 11, 13, 15, 17, 20, 32, 135
President of UNCTAD, 88, 109, 115

Regional arrangements (groupings), 34, 40-47, 52, 70, 76, 80, 92, 104, 116-117, 135

Secret diplomacy, 15, 17, 30, 31
Secretary General of UNCTAD, 83, 87-90, 93, 95, 98, 109,
    118, 121, 122, 124, 129, 130
Selection of diplomats, 5, 10, 12, 19
South-East-Asia Treaty Organization (SEATO), 43
Sovereignty, 26, 33, 34, 39, 43-44, 46, 64, 119
Special United Nations Fund for Economic Development
    (SUNFED), 75-76
Synthetics and substitutes, 51, 92, 95-96, 98

Trade and Development Board, 115, 117, 120, 124
Training of diplomats, 8, 12, 13, 19, 134
Treaty of Versailles, 14, 40, 68, 134

United Nations, 22, 32-40, 42, 43, 51, 68, 69-70, 75, 77,
    96, 102, 104, 116, 121, 127, 129, 133, 136
        Center for Industrial Development, 110
        Charter, 35, 36, 37, 38, 39, 40, 42, 104, 106, 117
        Economic and Social Council, 34, 38, 40, 69-74, 78,
            81-83, 109, 118, 128
            ECA, 70
            ECAFE, 70
            ECE, 70
            ECLA, 70
        General Assembly, 35, 36, 37, 39, 43, 69-70, 74, 77,
            81, 82, 106, 109, 111, 116, 118, 119, 120, 122,
            123, 124, 134
        International Court of Justice, 38
        Preparatory Committee, 36
        Secretariat, 39
        Secretary General, 35, 50, 55, 74, 78, 84, 88, 98,
            108, 119, 120, 122, 131
        Security Council, 35, 36, 37
        Technical Assistance, 75
United Nations Relief and Rehabilitation Administration
    (UNRRA), 67
Universal Postal Union, 28, 40, 67, 71

Yalta Conference, 35

ABOUT THE AUTHOR

Kamal M. Hagras has served as Consul of
the United Arab Republic in New York and has
held various diplomatic posts in a number of
different countries, giving him the opportunity
of observing the international scene firsthand.
He wrote this book under a fellowship from the
Rockefeller Foundation while on a leave of absence from government service. Dr. Hagras
holds a Ph.D. degree from New York University.